B-17 FLYING FORTRESS UNITS
OF THE EIGHTH AIR FORCE (PART 1)

SERIES EDITOR: TONY HOLMES

OSPREY COMBAT AIRCRAFT • 18

B-17 FLYING FORTRESS UNITS
OF THE EIGHTH AIR FORCE (PART 1)

Martin Bowman

OSPREY
AVIATION

Front cover
Famed Hollywood film director
William Wyler was sent to England
in late 1942 to make a documentary
– principally for American cinema
audiences – about the operations of
the Eighth Air Force. He began film-
ing early in 1943 following delays for
bad weather, and during the course
of shooting footage for the docu-
mentary, no less than five combat
photographers were lost on opera-
tions aboard B-17s.

By the spring of 1943, several
Flying Fortress crews from the 91st
Bombardment Group (BG), based at
Bassingbourn (Station 121) in
Cambridgeshire, were running neck
and neck for the honour of being the
first to complete 25 missions – the
length of a combat tour for aircrew
at that time. One clutch of airmen
who featured particularly prominent-
ly in Wyler's lens was the crew of
B-17F-10-BO 41-24485, better known
as the "MEMPHIS BELLE".

The director was almost certainly
drawn to this aircraft by its emotive
name and eye-catching nose-art,
which had been inspired by a Miss
Margaret Polk of Memphis,
Tennessee. The sweetheart of the
bomber's Captain, Robert K Morgan,
Miss Polk had been introduced to
the former whilst visiting her sister
in Walla Walla, Washington, where
Morgan was undertaking his crew
training. The romance between the
pilot and the Memphis 'belle' flour-
ished, but when Morgan was posted
to England their relationship eventu-
ally ended. However, the Boeing
'BELLE would become legendary.

The crew flew the 25th, and final,
mission of their tour on 17 May 1943
when they were part of a large force
sent to the French coastal city of
Lorient to bomb U-boat pens. Parts
of this mission were duly recorded
on 16 mm colour film and used to
great effect in the final documentary.
Although Morgan and his men had
not been sent to bomb a target deep
in Occupied Europe, this mission
proved to be anything but a 'milk
run' for the crew of the "MEMPHIS
BELLE". Having made it to the target
and dropped their load of 1000-lb GP
(General Purpose) bombs, they
swung the bomber north and head-
ed back over Brittany and out across
the Channel.

Leaving the French coast behind
them, and with the most dangerous

part of their 25th mission seemingly
over, the crewmen were on the
verge of celebrating their survival
when their formation was attacked
by a handful of Bf 109G-6s scrambled
from Morlaix. These fighters were
from 2./JG 2, and although they
pressed home their attacks, the
"MEMPHIS BELLE" survived
unscathed. This specially-commis-
sioned painting by Iain Wyllie shows
the American bomber defending
itself against the intercepting
Messerschmitt fighters, one of which
(G-6 Wk-Nr 15297, flown by Gunther
Krus) was shot down some 30 miles
north of Morlaix.

Having completed 25 missions in
the European Theater of Operations
(ETO), *"MEMPHIS BELLE"* and its

First published in Great Britain in 2000
by Osprey Publishing, Elms Court, Chapel Way, Botley, Oxford, OX2 9LP

© 2000 Osprey Publishing

ISBN 1 84176 021 8

Edited by Tony Holmes
Page design by TT Designs, T & B Truscott
Cover Artwork by Iain Wyllie
Aircraft Profiles and Nose-art by Mark Styling
Scale Drawings by Mark Styling
Origination by Grasmere Digital Imaging, Leeds, UK
Printed through Bookbuilders, Hong Kong

00 01 02 03 04   10 9 8 7 6 5 4 3 2 1

EDITOR'S NOTE
To make this best-selling series as authoritative as possible, the editor would be interested in hearing from any individual who may have relevant photographs, documentation or first-hand experiences relating to aircrews, and their aircraft, of the various theatres of war. Any material used will be credited to its original source. Please write to Tony Holmes at 10 Prospect Road, Sevenoaks, Kent, TN13 3UA, Great Britain, or by e-mail at: tony.holmes@osprey-jets.freeserve.co.uk

ACKNOWLEDGEMENTS
Assistance in the preparation of this volume was received from the following individuals: Mike Bailey, Cyrus R Broman, Tom Cushing, Joe D'Angelo, Bill Donald, Thomas J Fitton, Robert M Foose, Lt Col Harry D Gobrecht, Larry Goldstein, Lucy Helme at BAT, Richard R Johnson, the late Howard E Hernan, Brian S McGuire, Walter 'Don' O'Hearn, Connie and Gordon Richards, Hans-Heiri Stapfer, Frank Thomas and Truett L Woodall Jnr.

CONTENTS

CHAPTER ONE

YANKEE DOODLE GOES TO WAR 6

CHAPTER TWO

SPREADING THE WEALTH 18

CHAPTER THREE

'BLACK THURSDAY' AND BEYOND 62

CHAPTER FOUR

'BIG WEEK' AND 'BIG B' 75

CHAPTER FIVE

FINAL VICTORY 85

APPENDICES 100
COLOUR PLATES COMMENTARY 104

ten-man crew became instant celebrities. Everyone, it seemed, wanted to meet them, and on 26 May they were introduced to their Majesties King George VI and Queen Elizabeth at Bassingbourn, followed by Gen Jacob Devers (Commander of US forces in Britain) and Lt Gen Ira Eaker (Commander of the Eighth Air Force). Both generals later returned to Bassingbourn on 9 June 1943 to bade *"MEMPHIS BELLE"* and its crew farewell as the bomber set off for the USA to take part in a war bond tour.

The documentary *The Memphis Belle* finally emerged in April 1944 as a colourful, and exciting, 38-minute masterpiece, giving American cinemagoers a timely reminder of the grim realities of the high altitude war being fought out thousands of miles away over Europe. By this time the number of missions required to complete a tour had risen to 35, whilst the possibility of attaining such a tally was even more remote than it had been in the 'dark days' of 1942-43. Britons saw the documentary for the first time in the winter of 1944-45.

Made famous by its starring film role, the *"MEMPHIS BELLE"* was used for crew training in Florida following the completion of its war bond work, before finally being retired to Altus Air Force Base, in Oklahoma, for scrapping in mid-1945. However, unlike the tens of of surplus aircraft turned into ingots in the late 1940s, B-17F-10-BO 41-24485 was bought by the Memphis City Fathers, who firstly had it displayed outside the city's National Guard Armory, and then at the local airport. Finally, in 1987, the weary bomber was fully restored and installed in its own specially-constructed pavilion at the Mud Island leisure complex in Memphis

YANKEE DOODLE GOES TO WAR

On 2 January 1942 the order activating the Eighth Air Force was signed by Maj Gen Henry 'Hap' Arnold, Commanding General, Army Air Forces (AAF). Six days later the US Army announced that VIII Bomber Command (BC) was to be established in England, and Arnold instructed Brig Gen Ira C Eaker to assist in the formation of a headquarters for the American air forces in Great Britain. Eaker was designated as commanding general of VIII BC, and one of his first duties was to help prepare the airfields and installations deemed necessary for its groups to operate from. He was also tasked with studying the methods of the Royal Air Force's Bomber Command.

In early February 1942 Eaker, and his 'advanced detachment' of just six men, left for England. Initially, he would set up his HQ at RAF Bomber Command headquarters at High Wycombe, in Buckinghamshire. Just a matter of days later, on 22 February, VIII BC was formally activated. Between 31 March and 3 April Eaker and his staff officers made a more detailed reconnaissance of the Huntingdon area, which had originally been considered by the RAF for the location of a new Bomber Command formation, before it turned its attention to creating additional stations in Lincolnshire and South Yorkshire. The airfield construction programme in Huntingdon had continued, however, and these bases would soon house B-17 Flying Fortresses of the 1st Bombardment Wing (BW).

On 3 February 1942 the 97th, 301st and 303rd BGs were formally activated. These B-17E groups, and the 92nd, activated on 1 March 1942, and two Liberator groups (the 44th and 93rd BGs – see *Osprey Combat Aircraft 15 - B-24 Liberator Units of the Eighth Air Force* for further details), formed the nucleus of the US heavy bombardment force in England.

Three B-17Es in the 97th BG, led by 41-2578 *Butcher Shop*, taxy out at Grafton Underwood. This particular aircraft later transferred to the 326th BS/92nd BG, before moving again to the 457th BG at Glatton on 3 March 1944. It was re-named *Big Tin Bird*, and at Kingscliffe was used as a hack for Lt Col Cy Wilson, CO of the 20th FG. The oldest B-17 in the Eighth Air Force, 41-2578 was salvaged on 6 August 1945 (*USAF*)

Title page spread
B-17E 41-9023 *YANKEE DOODLE* was first assigned to the 92nd BG at MacDill Field on 13 March 1942. On 11 May the aircraft was transferred to the 414th BS/97th BG, and once in England it was one of 12 E-models that took part in the Eighth Air Force's first B-17 mission of the war, flown on 17 August 1942. Piloted by John Dowswell, it carried Brig Gen Ira C Eaker to Rouen. Seven days later, 41-9023 returned to the 92nd BG, where it served until 31 March 1943, when it joined the Blind Approach Training (BAT) Flight at Bassingbourn. In August 41-9023 was transferred again, this time to the 322nd BS/91st BG, and it ended its ETO service with the 324th BS as a target tow and general liaison aircraft. 41-9023 was finally salvaged on 26 July 1945 (*USAF*)

B-17E 41-9019 *"LITTLE SKUNK-FACE"* of the 414th BS/97th BG in early RAF-style camouflage. This E-model transferred to the 305th BG on 6 November 1942, and was later used by the 381st BG in June 1943. The following month it went to the 327th BS/92nd BG, where it served as a target tug. On 27 August 1943 it made its last move within the front-line force, being passed on to the 482nd BG at Alconbury. 41-9019 was finally written off on 21 August 1945 (*USAF*)

Some of the first AAF personnel to arrive in the UK were passengers aboard the ocean liner *Queen Elizabeth*, which dropped anchor in the Firth of Clyde on the morning of 9 June. Amongst the several thousand troops that disembarked were men from the 97th BG. Like all heavy bomb groups assigned to the ETO, this outfit consisted of four squadrons – the 340th, 341st, 342nd and 414th Bombardment Squadrons (BSs). Men of the 340th and 341st travelled to their new base at Polebrook (Station 110), in Northamptonshire, whilst personnel from the 342nd and 414th were sent a little further west to Grafton Underwood (Station 106), again in Northamptonshire.

Their B-17s, meanwhile, were not scheduled to fly in from Dow Field, Maine, and Grenier Field, New Hampshire, via the Northern Ferry Route, until mid-June. However, the bombers were delayed by the Japanese threat in the Aleutians (the 97th BG was temporarily placed on detached duty with Western Defence Command). By 23 June the enemy offensive had been halted, and the 97th returned to Presque Island, Maine, for the flight to England. Their route would be via Goose Bay, in Labrador, Bluie West 1, in Greenland, the Icelandic capital of Reykjavik and Prestwick, in Scotland.

On 26 June the first 15 B-17Es to attempt the crossing set off, but after departing Goose Bay on the second leg of the trip they encountered bad weather in Greenland and were forced to turn back. Eleven of the B-17s returned to Labrador after having been in the air for over 14 hours, whilst three other crews crash-landed in Greenland after flying into a snowstorm. None of the crewmembers was hurt, however, and they were quickly rescued. Astonishingly, the final B-17 actually managed to land in Greenland, at Bluie West 8 landing-ground, some 400 miles further east of its original destination.

On 1 July 1942 B-17E *Jarring Jenny* became the first Flying Fortress assigned to VIII BC to actually land in the UK when she flew into Prestwick. Three days later the following entry was made at High Wycombe – 'Arrival of aircraft: 1 B-17E. Total 1.'

In August the 97th BG was joined by the 92nd BG at Bovingdon (Station 112), in Hertfordshire, and the 301st BG at Chelveston (Station 105) and Podington (Station 109), both in Northamptonshire. All three groups had been hastily formed in the turbulent weeks following Pearl Harbor, and their training was incomplete. Some of the air gunners had

actually received little or no training in aerial gunnery, whilst the radio operators were in no better shape, being unable to send or receive morse signals. Finally, many of the pilots sent to the ETO had no experience of high altitude or formation flying.

Many crews, untrained as they were, had only just become familiar with their equipment, and each other, when they were pitched headlong into an air war senior AAF officers naively thought they could successfully wage in daylight, without fighter escorts. But the pressure was on VIII BC to show the British just what the Eighth Air Force could do.

At the end of July Col Frank A Armstrong, a 'West Pointer', and one of Eaker's original six staff officers at VIII BC HQ that had accompanied him to England in February, took over command of the 97th BG, which was under-performing, from Col Cornelius W Cousland. A tough, no-nonsense North Carolinian, erect in bearing and with a wind-tanned face (he had spent 14 of his 39 years in the cockpits of military aircraft), Armstrong commanded respect.

He turned the 97th around in short order, effectively taking the group apart and putting it back together again in just over two weeks! By mid-August, he was able to report to VIII BC HQ that 24 crews were available for daylight combat missions. The group's Executive Officer, Maj Paul W Tibbets (who later commanded the B-29 that dropped the atomic bomb on Hiroshima in August 1945), was to play a crucial part in this reorganisation and training. He later recalled;

'The seven weeks of training between our arrival in England and our first raid paid off handsomely. I shudder to think of the results had it not been for the intensive practice afforded during this period. In the States, we had learned to fly the B-17, and that was about it. The bombardiers and gunners arrived in England with insufficient training. The RAF people recognised this too, and were helpful in getting us ready for combat. Their fighters were sent up day after day so that we could practice rendezvous procedures with escort aircraft. The RAF even got some planes into the air to act as targets so that our gunners could develop the skills required to fire their weapons and operate turrets in combat.

'For all their help, however, we soon learned that it would have made more sense to provide this training over the broad expanse of Texas, and other western states, instead of trying to cram our learning experience into the limited airspace over England. Crews arriving in Europe later in the war would be better trained before leaving the US.'

The Eighth Air Force was fully committed to daylight bombing, despite doubts in many quarters. One critic was the air correspondent for *The Sunday Times*, Peter Masefield, who on 16 August wrote that 'American heavy bombers – the latest Fortresses and Liberators – are fine flying machines, but they are not suited for bombing in Europe. Their bombs and bomb loads are too small, their armour and armament are low'. He went on to suggest that the Fortress was more suited for flying anti-U-boat patrols over the Atlantic. Masefield was about to be made to eat his words, for just 24 hours after later the first VIII BC B-17 mission of the war took place.

FIRST MISSION

Col Armstrong and Maj Tibbets, flying in B-17E 41-2578 *Butcher Shop*, led the main group of 12 aircraft from Grafton Underwood in a raid on the Rouen Sotteville marshalling yards, in north-western France. Another six B-17Es from Polebrook acted as a diversionary force, heading for St Omer. Gen Eaker joined John Dowswell's crew in *Yankee Doodle* (414th BS B-17E 41-9023), which led the second flight of six in the main force. There were no aborts, and the RAF escort of four Spitfire Mk IX squadrons formed into an ad hoc wing gave the bomber crews both protection and comfort. Eaker recalled soon after the mission;

'Four squadrons of Spitfires tacked on – a flight on either side – at our level and about 400 yards to port and starboard. Thus escorted, we began the run across the Channel. There were still no clouds above or below, and visibility was virtually unlimited. From mid-Channel we could see the enemy coast rising in the distance as England's shores faded away behind. When we made landfall – at precisely the point indicated in our flight plan – all combat crewmen took up their stations. They seemed alert and vigilant. Our planes were in excellent formation, but perhaps not quite as tight as would have been ideal for protection against enemy attacks.'

At Ypreville enemy fighters (Fw 190s from II./JG 26 and JG 2) made their first appearance, and Sgt Adam R Jenkins, tail gunner aboard *Bat Outa Hell*, which was flying in the dreaded 'tail-end Charlie' slot in the formation, had his hands full. He later reported back at base;

'There were eight of them in "V" formation, and the leader waggled his wings and came for us. When they were about 300 yards away I figured it was about time for me to do something. So I pulled the trigger and it looked like the ends of his wings came off. Then the other seven scattered.'

One of these fighters flew straight into the line of fire of Sgt Kent R West's ball turret guns in the belly of 414th BS B-17E 41-9100 *Birmingham Blitzkrieg*. West opened up with his twin .50-cal guns, and his aim proved to be so accurate that he became the first American crewman to be credited with the destruction of a German aircraft upon his return to base. Altogether, two of the attacking fighters were shot down and five more claimed as 'probables' (only a single Fw 190 from JG 2 was actually destroyed, this falling victim to the B-17s' defensive fire) for the loss of two escorting Spitfires, and a third badly damaged.

The 12 Fortresses had dropped their 45 600-lb and nine 1100-lb British bombs on the locomotive and rolling-stock repair shops from

9

Parade for the award of Purple Hearts to wounded men of the 97th BG. Standing second from right is Lt Lockhart, with his hand bandaged as a result of the wounds he suffered on the mission of 24 August 1942 to Le Trait. Maj Tibbets is on his right, facing the camera (*Paul Tibbets Collection*)

23,000 ft, and although a few bombs struck a mile short of the target and several others exploded about a mile west in nearby woods, the majority struck the designated target area. Maj Tibbets recalls;

'We caught the Germans by surprise. They hadn't expected a daytime attack, so we had clear sailing to the target. Visibility was unlimited, and all 12 planes dropped their bombloads. Our aim was reasonably good, but you couldn't describe it as pinpoint bombing. We still had a lot to learn. A feeling of elation took hold of us as we winged back across the Channel. All the tension was gone. We were no longer novices at this terrible game of war. We had braved the enemy in his own skies and were alive to tell about it.'

All the B-17Es returned safely, and Gen Spaatz, elated with the success of the mission, stated 'I think the crews behaved like veterans. Everything went according to plan'. Col Armstrong went further, declaring 'We ruined Rouen'. This was clearly an exaggeration, but the first raid had seemed to verify the soundness of the AAF's policy of precision bombing of strategic objectives, rather than mass-bombing large city-sized areas.

In the wake of the mission the first of the congratulatory messages to arrive came from Air Marshal Sir Arthur Harris, Commander-in-Chief RAF Bomber Command;

'Congratulations from all ranks of Bomber Command on the highly successful completion of the first all-American raid by the big fellows on German-occupied territory in Europe. *Yankee Doodle* certainly went to town and can stick yet another well-deserved feather in his cap.'

On 19 August the 97th BG despatched 24 B-17Es in support of the Allied landings at Dieppe. Their target was the airfield at Abbeville-Drucat in northern France, home of JG 26, dubbed the 'Abbeville Kids' by Allied aircrews. Between 1940 and mid-1943, the pilots from this *Geschwader* enjoyed an almost mythical reputation (see *Osprey Aircraft of the Aces 9 - Fw 190 Aces on the Western Front* for more details).

Two of the B-17s aborted because of mechanical failures, but the rest of the group bombed the airfield, destroying a hangar and cratering the runways. The Luftwaffe, which was already heavily engaged to the southwest over Dieppe, did not show. The BBC Home Service report said that 16 fighters were either destroyed or damaged on the ground as a result of the bombing, and the airfield itself was put out of action for two hours. However, official German records reveal that only two Fw 190s were slightly damaged, and the airfield remained operational.

The following day 11 Fortresses of the 340th and 342nd BSs bombed the Longueau marshalling yards in Amiens through light flak. Again, RAF Spitfires protected the formation, and a Belgian fighter pilot who witnessed the raid reported that the bombers had scored at least 15 direct hits. On the 21st Fortresses set out for the Rotterdam Wilton shipyards. Slow to form up after leaving Grafton Underwood, the bombers were barely airborne when one B-17 was forced to abort – a replacement aircraft was quickly found. Three other B-17s also suffered mechanical problems such as generator failures, which caused the gun turrets to become inoperative. They too returned to base.

Running 16 minutes late for their escort, the remaining crews knew the short-ranged fighters (including Spitfires from the 31st FG's 308th FS) would not be able to stick with them all the way to the target. The Dutch coast was in sight when the recall message came through and the Spitfires turned for home. They were immediately replaced by around 25 fighters from II./JG 1, who attacked the now 'escortless' Fortresses for the next half-an-hour.

The crew of B-17F-10-BO 41-24444 *The Red Gremlin* (340th BS/97th BG) pose for a group photograph on 9 September 1942. 'Their' bomber had been delivered to the 97th BG on 2 July 1942, having been flown to England by Lt Charles N Austin. It was re-named *Superman* when it was assigned to the 92nd BG on 24 August. Seenin the back row, from left to right, are Maj Paul W Tibbets, Ryan, Tom W Ferebee, 'Dutch' Van Kirk, Hughes and Splitt. In the front row, again from left to right, are Peach, Quate, Fitzgerald, Gowan, and Fittsworth. On 17 August 1942 Tibbets used 41-2578 *Butcher Shop*, and Lt Butcher's crew, to lead the first Fortress raid of the war with his CO, Col Frank A Armstrong Jr. Three years later, Tibbets, his bombardier Tom Ferebee, and navigator 'Dutch' Van Kirk, flew in the same positions in B-29 *Enola Gay* on the first atomic bomb drop, on Hiroshima, Japan, on 6 August 1945. 41-24444 returned to the US in July 1944, and was salvaged on 19 June 1946 (*Paul Tibbets Collection*)

Surprised initially by the ferocity of the return fire from the tight formation of B-17s, five Fw 190 pilots instead chose to single out *Johnny Reb*, which was lagging behind the main formation. The bomber was hit in the cockpit by a 20 mm shell, exploding the Plexiglas windscreen and killing the co-pilot, 2Lt Donald A Walter. A flash fire also erupted behind the shattered instrument panel and seriously burned the hands of the pilot, 2Lt Richard S Starks.

Despite great pain, Starks managed to call for help over the intercom, and Walter's body was duly removed by bombardier 2Lt Edward T Sconiers and gunner Sgt Allen. Sconiers then took his place at the controls and nursed *Johnny Reb* back to East Anglia, where he performed a successful landing at the RAF Mosquito base at Horsham St Faith (Station 123), near Norwich.

The press enthusiastically reported that the the nine Fortress crews had destroyed six fighters, and praised them for beating off 25 Fw 190s – the Germans claimed one bomber damaged, and in turn recorded that a Focke-Wulf had been damaged by enemy fire. Despite the AAF not losing a single B-17 on this mission, some RAF officers remained unconvinced about unescorted daylight bombing. Their scepticism was further heightened when it later transpired that only a handful of fighters had actually fired on the formation. The bulk of the German pilots had been unpleasantly surprised by the defensive firepower of the new adversaries, and had duly kept their distance.

Late in the afternoon of 24 August a dozen 97th BG B-17Es, led by Maj Tibbets, attacked a shipyard at Le Trait, on the lower Seine. Twelve of the 48 bombs dropped fell within 500 yards of the aiming point, but seemingly no material damage was done to the yards. One wayward bomb luckily hit and sank a U-boat tied to the docks, but overall the bombing accuracy from this mission was the poorest to date. Flak in turn caused damage to the Fortresses, and five crewmen received slight wounds.

On the way home the formation was jumped from twelve o'clock by 'yellow-nosed' Bf 109Gs and Fw 190s (JG 26 and an attached *Staffeln* of JG 2 were involved), which were quickly engaged by the escorting Spitfire wing. On the fighters' opening pass, Tibbets' B-17E was hit in the cock-

Sometimes B-17s were lucky to make it back at all (*via Robert M Foose*)

pit by a 20 mm cannon shell, Plexiglas debris from the exploding round badly lacerating co-pilot Lt Gene Lockhart's hand, which in turn sprayed blood over what few instruments remained operable. Tibbets struggled with the controls, and somehow managed to keep the B-17E on course for home, despite the whole airframe shuddering from repeated cannon and machine gun strikes.

Once again, despite the best efforts of the German fighters, all the bombers returned to Grafton Underwood, where a ceremony was hastily arranged soon after the mission to allow Gen Spaatz to present Purple Hearts to those who had been wounded.

With the weather continuing to hold, bombing missions came thick and fast. On 27 August nine Fortresses paid a return visit to the Wilton shipyards in Rotterdam, which had been quickly restored to full capacity in the wake of the raid just six days earlier. Although only seven of the B-17s succeeded in dropping their bombs, hits were claimed on two ships, and the centre of the target was reported to have been 'well covered'. Twenty-four hours later the 97th sent 14 B-17s to the Avions Potez factory at Meaulte, in northern France. Due to poor bomb-aiming, most of the bombs dropped by the 11 Fortresses which reached the target fell in open fields, although some did crater the runways at an adjoining airfield.

In the last raid of the month, on the 29th, 12 B-17Es bombed the German fighter base at Coutrai-Wevelghem, in Belgium. The aircraft appeared over the target having somehow escaping detection by radar, and dropped their bombs in a concentrated pattern from 23,000 ft. Considerable damage was inflicted on the airfield, and a number of personnel were killed. No bombers were lost.

Es FOR Fs

With missions set to increase, and units starting to suffer attrition, Gen Eaker quickly realised that he needed a Combat Crew Replacement and Training Center (CCRC). However, personnel and equipment were in such short supply that the 92nd BG at Bovingdon was selected to fill this role, and they were withdrawn from combat. As a result their brand new B-17Fs were transferred to the 97th BG, and in return they received the latter group's battle-weary B-17Es! As the 11th CCRC, the group undertook this vital role for the next eight months.

On 5 September 25 of the 97th's newly-acquired B-17Fs, and for the first time 12 Fortresses from the 301st BG (which was flying its first combat mission of the war), were despatched to the marshalling yards at Rouen. Thirty-one B-17s bombed, the remaining six aborting with various mechanical problems. Of the bombs dropped, only 20 per cent actually fell within the target area, with some bombs hitting the city itself. Unconfirmed reports claimed that 140 French civilians were killed, with about 200 more being wounded. One bomb, which fortunately proved to be a dud, actually struck the city's main hospital, passing through several floors before burying itself in the basement.

Undeterred by this poor display, Eaker mounted his largest mission to date late the following afternoon, bombing the Avions Potez factory at Meaulte once again. In order to place as many 'heavies' over the target as possible, the 92nd BG was called into action for the first time – the group scraped together 14 B-17Es and crews, the latter being brought up to strength with ground personnel. They joined 22 B-17Fs of the 97th BG in the main strike on the factory, while the 301st flew a diversionary raid on St Omer-Longueness airfield.

Of the 30 Fortresses that made it to Meaulte, only eight were 92nd BG aircraft – four had aborted. Between 45 and 50 Fw 190s from JGs 2 and 26 intercepted the bombers as soon as they flew over the coast, the 'heavies' initially lacking any fighter cover due to the escorting Spitfire wing (including No 133 'Eagle' Sqn) having missed its rendezvous with the Fortresses. The first aircraft lost was 340th BS/97th BG B-17F 41-24445, flown by 2Lt Clarence C Lipsky. The bomber crashed in the vicinity of Flasselles, near Amiens, although four parachutes were seen to open behind the stricken bomber, which went down apparently under control followed by five fighters. Lipsky and five of his crew subsequently became Prisoners of War (PoWs).

At 6.55 pm on 6 September 1942, the Eighth Air Force had lost its first 'heavy' to the enemy (credited to II./JG 26 *Gruppenkommandeur* Hauptmann H K Conny Meyer – this was his tenth kill), and the second to fall would crash into the Channel less than 15 minutes later.

Having dropped its bombs and turned for home, 92nd BG B-17E *Baby Doll*, piloted by 2Lt Leigh E Stewart, was chased across the Channel by five Fw 190s again from II./JG 26. Badly shot up, the aircraft made it to within sight of Beachy Head, but eventually crashed into the water at 7.06 pm. RAF Air-Sea Rescue (ASR) launches were immediately despatched from Dover to search for survivors, but no trace of the crew, or their aircraft, was ever found. Oberfeldwebel Willi Roth of 4.*Staffel* was credited with the B-17's destruction, taking his tally to 17 kills.

Another bomber badly shot up whilst heading back to England was the 92nd BG B-17E flown by Capt Frank G Ward, which came under attack from six Fw 190s over Cayeaux-sur-Mer. One of the fighters fired several cannon rounds into the rear fuselage and tail of the aircraft, killing two gunners and wounding three others. A gunner in the 97th BG was killed and three more wounded in other shot up B-17s, one of the crewmen succumbing to his injuries in hospital three days later.

The loss of two B-17s and 18 aircrew was a major blow felt by all AAF personnel. The fatalities suffered by the essentially non-operational 92nd BG were particularly hard to accept, for the group had only flown on the 6 September mission because VIII BC had been so desperately short of aircraft and personnel to conduct this maximum effort.

This constant drain on the Eighth's precious resources was a direct result of the need to supply the Twelfth Air Force, which was destined to participate in Operation *Torch* – the invasion of North Africa, planned for 8 November. When the time came, both the 97th and 301st BGs would fly to North Africa and operate with the Twelfth, but in the meantime the two pioneer Fortress groups continued to fly with VIII BC.

On 7 September the B-17s bombed the shipyards in Rotterdam once again, although a storm warning that was flashed while they were outbound saw most crews return home early. However, seven aircraft within the 97th BG formation failed to receive the warning and pressed on to the target. They were swiftly engaged by Fw 190s from III./JG 26 and JG 1, who in turn were intercepted by the escorting Spitfire Mk IX wing.

Despite the efforts of the defending RAF fighters (which downed three Fw 190s of JG 1), the B-17F flown by Capt Aquilla Hughes was singled out by the German pilots. Enduring a series of attacking passes, during which the ball turret gunner was killed and three other gunners were wounded, the bomber somehow remained airborne on just two engines. Oil, and hydraulic lines and brakes were shot out, and the radio also began malfunctioning. Hughes had little choice but to drop out of formation and make his own way home as best he could. Amazingly, he nursed the aircraft back to base, landing sometime after the remaining six B-17s had all safely returned.

NEW GROUPS

Whilst the pioneer B-17 units were enduring their baptism of fire over occupied Europe, four new groups – the 91st, 303rd, 305th (which was commanded by the legendary Lt Col Curtis E LeMay) and the 306th BGs – were completing their final training in the USA. The 91st BG (commanded by Col Stanley T Wray) commenced flying across the Atlantic in September, but the group would have to wait until early October before it had enough B-17s on strength to mount its first mission.

The 306th (commanded by Col Charles 'Chip' Overacker) also departed for the UK in September, with the 303rd and 305th completing the crossing the following month. Once in England, these groups took time to adjust to their new surroundings, and it was not until November that Eaker could call upon them to provide aircraft and crews for the bombing offensive.

The 91st was allocated Kimbolton (Station 117), in Huntingdonshire, and the 303rd, 305th and 306th were sent to Molesworth (Station 107), also in Huntingdonshire, Grafton Underwood, in Northamptonshire, and Thurleigh (Station 111), in Bedfordshire.

Personnel of the 91st BG, nicknamed 'Wray's Wragged Irregulars', were not impressed with their new base, which was a typical wartime airfield consisting of unheated Nissen huts scattered over a vast open (and usually muddy) field. Built for RAF medium bombers, Kimbolton's runways soon proved to be neither long enough or strong enough for the AAF's B-17s, and only three practice missions were flown by the 91st before the unit decamped with all 32 of its B-17Fs to Bassingbourn (Station 121), in Cambridgeshire, on 14 October. This airfield was a pre-war RAF station with permanent runways, solid-brick buildings and comfortable messes.

B-17F-20-BO 41-24504 *THE SAD SACK* of the 324th BS/91st BG, along with sister-ship B-17F-20-BO 41-24505 *"QUITCHURBITCHIN"*, were the longest-serving of the Group's original 'Forts'. *"QUITCHURBITCHIN"* was battle damaged on its sixth mission, to St Nazaire, on 22 November 1942, and for a year it was used as a 'hangar queen', prior to being restored to flying condition. Transferred to Air Force Service Command (AFSC) at the end of 1943, the bomber was employed as a trainer before returning to the ZOI in June 1944. *THE SAD SACK* also returned to the USA in the spring of 1944, where it took part in a War Bond tour (*USAF*)

The new bomb groups' arrival meant changes in administration and accommodation for VIII BC. It was decided that from now on each group would base all four of its squadrons on one airfield. Accordingly, the 97th BG's 342nd and 414th BSs vacated Grafton Underwood and moved east to Polebrook to rejoin the 340th and 341st BSs, while the incoming 305th BG took over the former base. Group commander, Col LeMay, remembered many years later;

'Thus we were installed temporarily at Grafton Underwood, which did duty as an emergency-ward reception centre. We wouldn't be there long, and we knew it, and we were glad of it because the runways were all wrong. And the fog was awful, and everybody moaned and wailed "So this is England?" One pilot sat in a '17 was contacted by the tower, who asked him, "Can you see the runway lights?". He replied, "Shit, I can't even see my co-pilot".'

While the four 'new' groups got to grips with their English bases, and the weather, the 92nd, 97th and 301st BGs continued to carry the war to the enemy. On 9 October Eaker at last had enough bombers to attack the locomotive, carriage and wagon works at Fives-Lille, in France. By including the Liberators of the 93rd BG and Fortresses of the 306th BG (making their combat debut over the continent), VIII BC was able to assemble an unprecedented 108 bombers for the raid – a figure that would not be bettered in the ETO for a further six months.

B-17s of the 306th BG joined aircraft from the 92nd, 97th and the leading 301st, with the B-24s falling in behind the Fortresses. Seven bombers of the 92nd BG aborted for technical reasons, whilst a handful of aircraft from the other groups also returned early. Finally, just 69 bombers hit their primary targets, and many of the bombs dropped failed to explode. The inexperienced 93rd and 306th BGs' placed most of their bombloads outside the target area, killing a number of French civilians. The actual traffic control of the bombers over the target area also proved to be poor, and some bombardiers never actually managed to get the target in their bombsights.

As with previous missions, the bombers were given extensive fighter cover, including AAF P-38s of the 1st FG. However, the tactics employed by Fighter Command, and its AAF equivalent, VIII FC, proved to be too unwieldy. The attacking Luftwaffe pilots, from II. and III./JG 26, were told to ignore the fighters and go straight for the bombers, who soon found themselves fighting for their lives.

The loss of so many bombers through mechanical and crew failures had seriously compromised the defensive qualities of the group formations, and this resulted in two B-17s being lost to enemy fire. The first Fortress downed was that flown by Capt John W Olson of the 306th BG's 367th BS. Nicknamed *Snoozy II*, the bomber was singled out by the 9th *Staffel* of III./JG 26, led by Oberleutnant Otto 'Stotto' Stamberger.

Just how poor the tactics employed by the escorting Allied fighters were during this mission is revealed by the fact that the attacking Fw 190 pilots reported being able to clearly see contrails caused by the P-38s and Spitfires above them as they carried out stern-aspect attacks on the 306th BG bomber. Shot out of its defensive formation, the stricken B-17 was subsequently finished off by Leutnant Stammberger, who lodged the following combat report once he had landed back at Coutrai-Wevelghem;

'Approached (the bombers) from the rear. Full throttle. The things just grew bigger and bigger. Opened fire much too early and broke away for fear of ramming the "barn doors" (B-17s). I was puzzled not to have scored any hits until I remembered the size of the beasts – wingspan 40 metres! Right, get in much closer, things won't start to happen too soon. Concentrate on the engines of the left wing. Third pass and both port engines are burning. Then a good burst into the starboard outer as she starts to slide left, losing altitude in wild spirals. At about 2000 metres four or five men manage to bale out before the crate hits the ground east of Vendeville.'

The second B-17 to be lost, from the 301st BG, made it part-way across the Channel before being forced to carry out the first successful ditching of a B-17 in the ETO. Most of its crew was soon rescued by RAF ASRs, although several fell into enemy hands. Hauptmann Klaus Mietusch, 7.*Staffel Kapitän*, was credited with the bomber's destruction.

Gunners had claimed 56 fighters destroyed, 26 probably destroyed and 20 damaged, which added up to more than the entire German defensive fighter force on the Channel front! These scores were finally whittled down to 21-21-15, although in reality only a single 7.*Staffel* Fw 190 had been lost – Unteroffizier Viktor Hager, flying as wingman to Hauptmann Mietusch, had been hit by machine gun fire during his *Staffel's* first pass at the Fortresses, and although he had baled out of his fighter, the severity of his wounds had prevented him from opening his parachute.

A further 11 missions scheduled for October were scrubbed due to poor weather, leaving the raid flown on the 21st against the U-boat base at Lorient as the only one to reach its designated target – a new directive issued by the Eighth Air Force 24 hours earlier had made U-boat facilities the top priority for VIII BC.

B-17E 41-9020 *PHYLLIS* was assigned to the 340th BS/97th BG at Polebrook in March 1942, and in August joined the 92nd BG at Bovingdon, making several courier flights to North Africa. In September 1942 *PHYLLIS* was involved in a collision with B-17E 41-9051 (from the 326th BS), although both bombers were repaired. On 1 May 1943 she was re-assigned to the 303rd BG at Molesworth and renamed *Tugboat Annie*. With Maj L M Schulstad at the controls, on 23 July 1944 the bomber suffered a crash-landing and was salvaged by the 2nd SAD at Little Staughton. In this photograph, taken early on in *PHYLLIS'* career, crewmen enjoy hot coffee and doughnuts out on the flightline, courtesy of an American Red Cross Clubmobile (*USAF*)

Altogether, 66 B-17s of the 97th, 301st and 306th BGs (along with 24 B-24s) were despatched, the bombers being split into two groups, led by the 97th BG group commander, Col Joseph H Atkinson. Following the losses of the previous raids, mission planners had drawn up a route which kept the bombers over the Bay of Biscay until the last possible moment to hopefully avoid the German fighters. As it turned out, thick cloud over Lorient at the prescribed bomb release altitude of 22,000 ft caused two-thirds of the force to abort the mission short of the target.

Only the 97th BG now remained on course, and once in the target area, Maj Joseph A Thomas, as lead pilot, guided the group through the undercast, breaking clear over Lorient at 17,500 ft. The German defenders were caught napping, and before the alarm could be sounded 2000-lb bombs were exploding in the target area, 21 falling within 1000 ft of the designated Mean Point of Impact (MPI).

Five bombs hit the central block of submarine pens, yet did not penetrate more than five feet into the structure. U-boat pens were poor targets for heavy bombers, being small in area and protected by reinforced concrete 16 ft thick! Indeed, a 1600-lb armour-piercing bomb dropped from 16,000 ft achieved sufficient impact velocity (about 860 ft per second) to penetrate just eight inches of armour. However, three general workshops and a pair of floating docks were destroyed, whilst two U-boats caught in the open received blast damage.

Having enjoyed the element of surprise over the target, the 97th BG turned for home. Just after re-crossing the French coast and heading north-east into the Bay of Biscay, the formation of 15 Fortresses was bounced by a swarm of Fw 190s. The German pilots (almost certainly from III./JG 2, which was based at Brest-Guipavas, and tasked with protecting the U-boats and their French bases) pressed home their attacks in such a manner that the high tails of the bombers actually shielded the fighters from firing positions in the radio hatch and top turret.

A series of ferocious passes was made on the rear of the formation, and three Fortresses succumbed to the incessant attacks. First to go down was *Francis X*, piloted by Lt Francis X Schwarzenbeck. Although he and his crew could have baled out of their stricken bomber, they chose to remain at their posts when they saw that they were flying headlong into another formation of German fighters. Guns blazing, *Francis X* managed to destroy two Fw 190s on its way down. *Johnny Reb*, flown by Lt Milton M Stenstrom, and another unnamed Fortress piloted by Capt John M Bennett were lost just minutes after *Francis X*, and six more shot-up bombers landed at bases on England's south coast.

The Fortress gunners claimed 10-4-3, but the 97th BG had by now suffered the highest losses of any unit to date. This mission proved to be the last flown from England by the group, for on 9 November it commenced a theatre move to North Africa, and the Twelfth Air Force. The 301st BG would follow 17 days later.

For three months the 97th and, to a lesser extent, the 301st BGs had pioneered American daylight bombing from England. Due to the sacrifices made by both units in combat, the air policy originally adopted by VIII BC when it commenced operations in August was extensively modified, and subsequent arrivals in England would benefit greatly from the changes brought about by the 'pioneer' bomb groups.

SPREADING THE WEALTH

Following the mauling of the 97th BG on the Lorient raid, and its subsequent departure, along with the equally battle-seasoned 301st, to North Africa, the future now looked bleak for the inexperienced groups that remained in England. Despite early successes, the Eighth Air Force still had to prove that high-altitude missions in daylight, often without escort, could justify further bomb groups being sent to the ETO. Shallow penetration missions, or 'milk-runs' as they began to be called, therefore became the order of the day – these were inspired by the good results achieved by the 97th BG, bombing at around 17,000 ft, in the same Lorient mission that had subsequently seen the group badly shot up on their return flight to England.

On 7 November VIII BC struck at the U-boat pens at Brest, on the French Atlantic coast, with a force of 54 B-17s. Fourteen of these aircraft came from the 91st BG (seven each from the 322nd and 324th BSs, including *"MEMPHIS BELLE"*), which was making its combat debut. Leading 'Wray's Wragged Irregulars' on this day was group commander, Col Stanley T Wray. The remaining bombers came from the 306th BG (24 aircraft) and 301st BG (16 B-17s). As the only operational group left in the ETO with any real combat experience (one mission!), the 306th was charged with leading the raid. A combination of poor weather and technical problems (frozen guns in the most part) resulted in few bombing successes, and for once the Luftwaffe made only sporadic attempts to engage the B-17s.

B-17Fs of the 303rd 'Hell's Angels' BG being bombed up at Molesworth. This group flew its first combat mission on 17 November 1942 (*USAF*)

Two days later VIII BC attacked the heavily defended U-boat base at St Nazaire. Pin-point accuracy was required against fortified blast pens, and in order to avoid radar detection the 47 B-17s and B-24s sent to attack the French port crossed the Channel at just 500 ft above the sea. Skirting around the Brest peninsula, they then climbed to between 7500 and 10,000 ft (the 12 B-24s continued climbing until they reached 18,000 ft) before running into the target. At this height the Boeing bombers ran the gauntlet of numerous light flak batteries – 20 mm and 37 mm – which had previously been ineffective against the high-flying 'heavies'.

Leading the attack were 13 B-17Fs of the 91st BG, which made their bombing run at 10,000 ft. All bar one aircraft was duly peppered with flak, which killed one crewman and seriously wounded two others. None of the B-17s was lost, however, but the 306th BG would not be so lucky. Running in behind the 91st at just 7500 ft, the group lost three B-17s in quick succession to the deadly accurate German flak gunners.

The final attacking run was made by the 12 B-24Ds of the 44th and 93rd BGs, who flew over the target at 18,000 ft. Well out of range of the flak batteries, the Liberators all returned to base with very little damage.

Although no fighters had been encountered on this mission due to the bombers coming in 'under the radar', the loss of three B-17s far outweighed any advantages gained from attacking at lower altitudes. From now on all VIII BC raids would be made from 'four miles high'.

Despite the results of the 9 November mission, the U-boat pens continued to feature prominently on target lists. To counter these frequent raids, the Germans moved in more heavy calibre anti-aircraft guns, and soon flak became as deadly at 20,000 ft as it had been at 7500 ft.

On 17 November the Fortresses headed back to St Nazaire, with 16 B-17s from the 303rd BG from Molesworth undertaking the group's maiden combat mission. Thick cloud obscured the target, however, and the group returned without dropping its bombs. Eager to make a contribution to the war effort, the 303rd despatched a further 19 Fortresses to attack U-boat pens at La Pallice, some 100 miles south of St Nazaire on the Atlantic coast. This time the group did get to drop their bombs, but on the previous day's target! Incredibly, the formation had veered some 100 miles off course en route to La Pallice.

The submarine pens at Lorient again came in for attention on 22 November, 76 bombers being despatched by VIII BC. Poor weather again hindered the attack, and only 11 B-17s from the 303rd BG, still smarting from its embarrassing navigational error four days before, actually succeeded in bombing the target through a gap in the cloud.

The following day St Nazaire was once again top of the target list, and the force sent to bomb the U-boat base included the 305th BG, which would be experiencing combat for the first time.

Post-mission photo-reconnaissance of VIII BC targets was revealing that a single bomb, or even a few bombs, failed to have enough destructive power to inflict any lasting damage – particularly on fortified targets such as U-boat pens. Ever the innovator, Col LeMay was determined to alter this, and he decided to try and achieve greater bombing accuracy by flying a straight course on the bomb run instead of zigzagging every ten seconds. The latter tactic was designed to spoil the aim of the flak batteries, but in reality only produced a scattered bombing pattern.

LeMay's plan called for the bombers to cross the target at greater rapidity, thus reducing the amount of time flak batteries had in which to take aim and fire on the formation. Conversely, this tactic increased the time the bombardier had to align his bombsight over the MPI. Championing such a drastic, and unproven, change was a big step for a group commander to take with such an inexperienced unit, and it greatly concerned his crews.

On 23 November 58 B-17s flew to Davidstowe Moor, in Cornwall, to refuel, before setting out on the long water crossing over the Atlantic and the Bay of Biscay to St Nazaire. Bad weather and mechanical problems forced 13 B-17s to abort well before the target, whilst a single Fortress, flown by 1Lt Clay Isbell of the 306th BG, was shot down by fighters on the bomb run. By the time the target was reached four out of the twenty B-17s in the 305th, five out of the ten 91st bombers and four out of the eight B-17s in the 306th had turned back. Only 44 B-17s remained, including five from the 91st and four from the 306th.

Despite this, both groups pressed on to the U-boat pens. Putting LeMay's tactics to the test, the 305th BG carried out the longest, and straightest, bomb run yet flown by VIII BC over Europe, and strike photos later revealed that the group had placed twice as many bombs on the target as any other outfit. Despite their fears, no crews were lost to flak, but the 91st and the 303rd BGs lost several B-17s to the new *Jagdwaffe* tactic of frontal assaults.

This deadly new tactic had been devised by veteran III./JG 2 *Gruppenkommandeur*, Oberleutnant Egon Mayer, a highly successful ace and master tactician (he had scored 102 kills on the western front by the time of his death in March 1944). He had quickly realised after his first few engagements with the 'mad Americans' that traditional attacks from the rear, or six o'clock low position, left the fighter pilot exposed to the various heavy calibre machine guns grouped around the rear of the aircraft. Despite approach angles being varied in an effort to reduce the effectiveness of these weapons, when the bombers maintained a close defensive formation they remained relatively safe from attack.

A detailed examination by the enemy of the few AAF 'heavies' that had fallen in France had revealed the lack of nose armament, so a number of *Jagdflieger* chose to attack the bombers head-on. Such a tactic involved great skill, as the pilot had to take effective aim as the fighter and bomber approached each other at a combined closing speed of almost 600 mph. Nerves of steel were also required due to the increased possibility of a mid-air collision. Mayer could see that head-on tactics was the way ahead, for not only would irreparable damage be done to the cockpit area of the bomber, it could force the pilot to take evasive action as the fighter closed on him. This would result in the much feared defensive formation being compromised, and the lone bomber placed at a greater risk of further attack.

Utilising these tactics on 23 November, III./JG 2 pilots attacked in flights of three. The Fw 190s first went after the four 91st BG B-17s which had made it to the target area. A fifth aircraft, B-17F 41-24479 *Sad Sack*, flown by 323rd BS CO, Maj Victor Zienowicz, had lost an engine soon after turning onto the final course for St Nazaire, forcing it to turn back for England. Neither the bomber, or its crew, was seen again.

All four B-17s in the formation were badly hit, with B-17F 41-24503 *Pandora's Box* losing two engines. Unable to keep up with the remaining bombers, the aircraft slowly dropped back as it limped over the Bay of Biscay. It was eventually lost with all hands, including the 324th BS CO, Maj Harold Smelser. Aside from losing two unit commanders, the 91st BG also lost the group navigator, bombardier and gunnery officers when these bombers crashed.

Of the three remaining Fortresses, only B-17F 41-24505 *"QUITCHURBITCHIN"* of the 324th BS succeeded in reaching Bassingbourn, where its pilot, Lt Charles E Cliburn, performed a successful landing despite the bomber's tailwheel hydraulics having been shot out. Capt Kenneth Wallick just reached RAF Chivenor, in Devon, in his severely damaged B-17, but sadly Lt Nathan N Corman, piloting 324th BS B-17F 41-24506 *The Shiftless Skunk*, was not so lucky. When he attempted a forced-landing near Watford, the bomber hit a 15-ft high high-tension pylon and crashed. Three crewmen died instantly and two later succumbed as a result of their wounds.

The final Fortress lost during the raid was 359th BS/303rd BG B-17F 41-24568 *Lady Fairweather*, flown by Capt Charles G Miller, which was set on fire near the target during a head-on pass. The bomber struggled back out to sea, before ditching in the Bay of Biscay.

RECTIFYING WEAKNESSES

The new head-on tactic (which led to the famous AAF warning 'bandits at twelve o'clock high') had cruelly exposed serious combat weaknesses in the defensive weaponry of the B-17E/F. Although some enterprising armament chiefs experimented with tail guns mounted in the nose of their bombers, the susceptibility of the Fortress to head-on attacks by the Luftwaffe would only be alleviated with the arrival of new G-models fitted with chin turrets. Eaker could not wait for the new aircraft with power-operated chin turrets, so the cycle of missions continued – weather and group reorganisation permitting.

Early in December the 305th BG moved south from Grafton 'Undermud' to Chelveston. That month the B-17s were scheduled to attack the steelworks at Lille-Fives on the 3rd, 5th and 6th, but bad weather saw

B-17F-27-BO 41-24585 *Wolf Hound* of the 360th BS/303rd BG became the first American bomber captured intact on 12 December 1942. Its pilot, 1Lt Paul F Flickinger, was forced to surrender the aircraft at Leeuwarden, in Holland, after being attacked by German fighters on the mission to the Rouen-Sotteville marshalling yards. *Wolf Hound* was tested at the Luftwaffe Test and Evaluation Centre at Rechlin, and in 1943 was issued to KG 200 for training and fighter affiliation duties (*Hans-Heiri Stapfer*)

bombs dropped on the latter date only. On this occasion the bombers were escorted by 16 Spitfire squadrons.

Attention then turned to the major Luftwaffe servicing facility at Romilly-sur-Seine, which carried out repair work, and prepared new aircraft, for *Luftflotte 3*. Situated on the banks of the Seine, south-east of Paris, the base was 100 miles further east than any target previously bombed by VIII BC. The first mission date for the Romilly-sur-Seine attack was 10 December, but this was cancelled due to heavy cloud over the target. Forty-eight hours later 90 bombers crossed the French coast when cloud again ruled out an attack on the servicing base.

The aircraft then changed course and attacked Rouen-Sotteville marshalling yards instead, although only a handful of B-17s from the 91st and 303rd BG's actually dropped any bombs. An estimated 30 Fw 190s intercepted the bombers, and two 303rd BG aircraft fell to the guns of Leutnant Otto 'Stotto' Stammberger's 9./JG 26.

A tired and drawn Capt Harold Stouse of the 359th BS/303rd BG, who piloted B-17F-27-BO 41-24635 *The 8 Ball Mark II* to Wilhelmshaven on 27 January 1943, fills out his flight report after the mission. This was the first time VIII BC had bombed a German target. On 18 March Stouse flew B-17F-25-BO 41-24561 *The Duchess* home to Molesworth with the body of 1Lt Jack W Mathis, lead bombardier, aboard. Mathis was awarded a posthumous Medal of Honor (the first awarded to an Eighth Air Force crewmember) for his actions this day on the mission to Vegesack (*USAF*)

One of the Fortresses lost was B-17F-27-BO 41-24585 *Wolf Hound* of the 360th BS, which put down in a Dutch field near Leeuwarden with only modest damage. This bomber later became the first of more than a dozen Fortresses restored to airworthiness by the Luftwaffe and flown for 'tactical evaluation and clandestine operations'.

Finally, on 20 December 101 bombers (the largest force despatched since the Lille-Fives raid of 9 October) made it to Romilly-sur-Seine. Twelve squadrons of RAF and AAF Spitfires had accompanied the bombers as far as Rouen, which was the extreme limit of the fighters' modest range. Once the last unit had swung back west, II. and III./JG 26 made their move. Both *Gruppen* had been shadowing the formation for quite some time, waiting for their escorts to depart.

The 91st BG in particular was badly hit in these early passes, losing two B-17s in quick succession. The first to fall was the 401st BS's 41-24432 *Danellan*, flown by Lt Dan W Carson. Only one crewman successfully baled out. The second bomber destroyed, B-17F 41-24452, was also from the 401st BS. Flown by Lt Robert S English, it crashed near Rouen with the loss of three crew. The destruction of these aircraft was credited to the two *Gruppenkommandeur*, Hauptmann H K Conny Meyer of II.*Gruppe* (the original AAF bomber 'killer', this was his 11th victory) and III.*Gruppe*'s legendary Maj 'Pips' Priller (taking his score to 81).

For the next hour the remaining 91st BG crews fought off a series of determined attacks until the Spitfire escort showed up to cover the bombers' exit across the Channel. Altogether, six B-17s (including four from the 306th) had been lost to the Fw 190s of II. and III./JG 26 and II./JG 2, with a further 31 damaged to varying degrees. German claims for this action totalled eight B-17s destroyed, five by JG 26 and three by JG 2. On the American side, AAF gunners once again submitted high claims, with their initial score of 53 'kills' being reduced to 21, and a further 31 'probably damaged'. Luftwaffe records reveal that JG 2 had two pilots shot down and killed and 1./JG 26 lost Feldwebel Heinz-Günther Adam when his fighter stalled on approach to Drucat – a second fighter from this *Staffel* was damaged by defensive fire. Six more Fw 190s were written off in forced-landings caused by a lack of fuel, while 11 others were deemed repairable.

Although 72 'heavies' had bombed the target, they had caused only minor damage to the German airfield. Despite this, the raid on Romilly-sur-Seine had proven a turning point in the daylight aerial war in Europe. For the first time VIII BC aircraft had penetrated 100 miles into enemy territory, successfully beating off incessant fighter attacks without the aid of escorting fighters.

IMPROVING PERFORMANCE

As 1942 drew to a close, the officers and men of VIII BC were still working on improving bombing and aerial gunnery. The two problems were indelibly linked, for an aircraft that was manoeuvring to avoid attack made for an unstable bombing platform. On the other hand, a bomber flying straight and level to the target when under attack from enemy fighters was effectively a sitting duck.

At Chelveston, Col LeMay worked harder than most to find the best method of combating fighter attacks without compromising bombing accuracy, and vice-versa. After trying 'stacked up' formations of 18 aircraft, he finally decided upon staggered three-bomber elements within a squadron, and staggered squadrons within a group. Such a formation resulted in a complicated bombing procedure if each B-17 tried manoeuvring for accurate aiming, so LeMay discarded individual bombing, which had been SOP (Standard Operating Procedure) from the outset.

Instead, he created 'lead crews', whose bombardier signalled to the rest of the formation when to drop their ordnance so that all bombs were released simultaneously, no matter what position the aircraft were flying in the group. At 1st BW HQ, the newly-arrived Brig Gen Larry Kuter, and his successor, Brig Gen Hayward 'Possum' Hansell, lent support to LeMay's theories, and gradually lead crews, comprising highly trained pilots, bombardiers and navigators, became SOP within VIII BC.

Tail unit of B-17F-25-BO 41-24569 *Memphis Tot* from the 427th BS/303rd BG. This aircraft, and Capt Lloyd R Cole's crew, failed to return from Emden on 4 February 1943 when they were shot down by fighters from IV./NJG 1 and crashed at Zwolle, eight kilometres north-east of Den Helder, in Waddensee, at 11.17 hours. Four of the crew were killed, whilst the remaining six survived to become PoWs (*Rob de Visser Collection via Theo Boiten*)

B-17F-27-BO 41-24639 *The CAREFUL VIRGIN*, which reached the 323rd BS/91st BG at Bassingbourn on 29 January 1943. On 7 May 1944 this aircraft was transferred to AFSC for *Aphrodite* missions. On 4 August 1944 41-24639 was packed with ten tons of nitro and used against a V-weapon site at Mimoyecques, in France. The bomber crashed 500 yards' short of the target and exploded (*USAF*)

The lead crew concept was first attempted on 30 December during a raid on Lorient, but head-on attacks by the Luftwaffe once again wrought havoc with the B-17 formation. Three bombers were lost, including 401st BS/91st BG B-17F 41-24449 *Short Snorter*, flown by Lt William T Bloodgood. None of the ten-man crew survived.

Three days into the New Year Gen Eaker completely abandoned individual bombing in favour of group bombing for the first time, VIII BC's target on this day being one of the most hated – St Nazaire. Altogether, 107 bombers were despatched, but mechanical failures saw many aircraft return to base early, leaving just eight B-24s and 68 B-17s to press on to the target. Visibility was unlimited, so an unusually long bomb run was ordered.

Aircraft were stacked upwards between 20,000 and 22,000 ft on the final run in to the submarine base, but progress was painfully slow for the bombers' groundspeed had been cut by more than half due to a 115 mph sub-stratosphere gale encountered on approach to the target. Indeed, the winds were so strong that the bomb run took twice as long as had been briefed, leaving the 'heavies' to fly straight and level for an agonising ten minutes as the flak gunners threw everything they could at them.

Prior to this mission, flak had not really worried VIII BC, for most shells could not reach 20,000 ft with any accuracy. However, much work had been done by flak batteries to perfect the firing of a box barrage at the target, and the extended bomb run gave the flak gunners ample time to correctly calculate the height at which to fire their barrage. Two B-17s were shot down over the target, and a third that failed to return was also judged to have been hit by flak. More than half of the bombers that did make it back to England suffered varying degrees of damage. A further four B-17s were downed by Fw 190s from III./JG 2, which claimed 15 destroyed in total.

Despite the flak and fighters, the 'heavies' had carried out the most accurate bomb drop of the war to date, with most of the 342 '1000 pounders' dropped hitting the U-boat pens. It appeared that Col LeMay's revised tactics worked, but at a cost – 70 men were missing from the seven bombers shot down, several more had been killed in crash-landings in England when the bombers ran out of fuel, and a further 47 B-17s had been damaged. Two 305th BG B-17s were damaged so severely that they were left in Wales where they had landed. These were the heaviest losses that VIII BC had suffered to date.

All the B-17 groups in the Eighth Air Force had been badly affected by the losses of the previous months, but one in particular seemed to be on the verge of falling apart. The 306th BG at Thurleigh, commanded by Col Charles B 'Chick' Overacker, had been in-theatre longer than any other Fortress group. Fiercely protective of his men, Overacker had protested vehemently when told to send his group over St Nazaire at just 7000 ft on 9 November. His objections were overruled, and two bombers were subsequently lost. Overacker had led his group that day, and his own bomber had returned to base badly shot up.

Aware of flagging morale at Thurleigh (the 306th had lost nine B-17s over its previous three missions), Gen Eaker paid a personal visit to the base the day after the 3 January raid on St Nazaire. He took

B-17F-25-BO 41-24561 *THE DUCHESS* of the 359th BS/303rd BG, which bombardier Jack Mathis manned on 18 March 1943 when his actions earned him a posthumous Medal of Honor (*via Mike Bailey*)

with him his A-3 (Operations and Training), Col Frank A Armstrong, who had led the 97th BG six months earlier. 'Things are not going well up there', he told the colonel. 'I think we ought to take a look around'.

The general's staff car was casually waved past at the main gate by a sentry who neither saluted, nor checked the occupants' identity. 'As we visited hangars, shops and offices', Eaker recalled, 'I found similar attitudes as seen at the front gate. The men had a close attachment to the CO, and he to them. But there was a lack of military propriety, and I could not help feel that this might be part of the problem that was being revealed in combat'.

Eaker relieved Col Overacker of his command on the spot and appointed Armstrong in his place. The new CO's stay would be short at just over a month, but he made his presence felt, working his new crews hard, and instilling badly needed discipline, especially in the air. In the classic war film *Twelve O'Clock High* (screenplay co-written by VIII BC staff officer Lt Col Beirne Lay and ex-AAF Maj Sy Bartlett), its central character was based on Col Armstrong, while the fictitious '918th BG' was derived by multiplying 306 by three.

While Armstrong was rebuilding the 306th BG, most of the 92nd BG moved north from Bovingdon to Alconbury (Station 102), in Huntingdonshire. It left behind numerous key personnel and all of the 326th BS, whilst other crews were sent to the 91st and 303rd BGs as 'temporary' replacements, although very few of these men ever returned to the 92nd.

On 13 January VIII BC again visited the locomotive works at Lille-Fives. As a result of the success of Col LeMay's tactics over St Nazaire ten days earlier, the lead slot for the formation fell to the 305th BG once more. The lead crew for the mission were from the 364th BS, flying B-17F *Dry Martini II*. This aircraft was normally flown by Capt Allen V Martini, but on this occasion the pilot's seat had been taken by squadron CO, Maj T H Taylor, due to the former being ill. Also along for his combat orientation flight was new 1st BW HQ commander, Brig Gen Hayward Hansell, who had relieved Brig Gen Larry Kuter on 3 January – Kuter had been posted to North Africa to serve on Gen Eisenhower's staff, becoming Deputy Commander.

All four B-17 groups adopted the staggered 18-aircraft bombing formation on this day, some 64 out of 72 Fortresses that set out making it to the target. Attacking at high altitude, the bombers were detected by

German radar well before they had crossed the French coast at Calais, allowing I. and III./JG 26 to take-off and form up for a series of passes on the 'heavies'. Adopting a line-astern tactical formation, flights of five or six Fw 190s intercepted the B-17s from head-on, attacking one at a time.

In the lead position, the 305th BG bore the brunt of the first passes. One Fortress was shot down, and a further ten, including *Dry Martini II*, which was hit in the cockpit by a single cannon shell, were damaged. Maj Taylor was struck in the chest by the round and killed instantly, whilst his co-pilot was wounded.

Two more Fortresses (from the 306th BG) suffered a mid-air collision over Belgium after completing their bombing run. AAF gunners claimed six fighters destroyed and 13 probably destroyed in reply, although German records reveal that not a single Fw 190 suffered reportable damage.

This mission proved to be one of the most successful flown by VIII BC to date. Aside from suffering minimal losses, the bombers had damaged their target so badly that AAF 'heavies' never needed to return to Lille-Fives. The lead bomber tactics devised by Col LeMay had proven their worth, and they became SOP from this day forth.

Despite the success of these early missions in 1943, there had been talk in various quarters suggesting that the handful of VIII BC groups should become part of RAF Bomber Command. Senior RAF officers felt that the Eighth Air Force had achieved only modest results at an ever increasing cost in men and machines, leaving few convinced that daylight attacks would ever succeed.

Gen 'Hap' Arnold, Chief of the American Air Staff, was also coming under increasing pressure from various quarters who wanted to know why Ira Eaker had been unable to mount more missions, and why it was French, rather than German, targets that were being bombed. Once again the future of VIII BC as a separate bombing force was in question, and answers were desperately needed if it was to survive.

GERMANY ATTACKED

In an attempt to answer the increasing chorus of critics on both sides of the Atlantic, Gen Eaker decided to send his command to attack Germany for the first time on 27 January 1943. A 64-strong force was sent to attack the U-boat construction yards at Vegesack, on the Weser, some 30 miles south of the North Sea coast.

RAF Bomber Command had attacked Vegesack four times in 1941-42, the most recent raid on the night of 23/24 September involving 24 Stirling bombers of No 3 Group. These missions had resulted in severe damage being caused to the town itself, and had destroyed a large naval ammunition dump. However, some of the U-boat slipways, dry-docks and shipyards had escaped damage, giving the Americans the ideal opportunity to prove that they could bomb Germany more effectively in daylight.

17 NOV	ST. NAZAIRE	14 FEB.	HAMM
18 NOV	ST. NAZAIRE	16 FEB.	ST. NAZAIRE
22 NOV	LORIENT	26 FEB.	WILHELMSHAVEN
23 NOV	ST. NAZAIRE	27 FEB.	BREST
6 DEC	LILLE	4 MAR.	ROTTERDAM
12 DEC	ROUEN	6 MAR.	LORIENT
20 DEC	ROMILLY	8 MAR.	RENNES
30 DEC	LORIENT	12 MAR.	ROUEN
3 JAN		13 MAR.	AMIENS
13 JAN		18 MAR.	VEGESACK
23 JAN	LORIENT	22 MAR.	WILHELMSHAVEN
27 JAN	VEGESACK	28 MAR.	ROUEN
4 FEB.		31 MAR.	ROTTERDAM

Mission list on the brick wall above the fireplace at the 303rd BG Officers' Club at Molesworth, showing the group's record during its first 26 combat missions (*Harry D Gobrecht via Brian McGuire*)

Knowing the importance of this mission, Eaker entrusted its leadership to Col Frank Armstrong, who had miraculously transformed the 306th BG into an efficient bombing 'machine' in just 23 days.

Despite predicted good conditions over the continent, cloud at bombing altitude soon thinned out the formation's ranks, and by the time the German coast came into view, only 55 Fortresses remained of the 64 that had taken off from Bassingbourn, Molesworth, Chelveston and Thurleigh. It was obvious to Armstrong that Vegesack would be totally obscured, so he turned his bombers instead towards the secondary target – the naval dockyard at Wilhelmshaven. The latter was also covered in cloud, although this was sufficient thin enough to allow 53 B-17s to drop their bombs almost blindly from 25,000 ft. Further adding to the obscurity of the target was a German smoke screen, which drifted lazily over the shipyards. The remaining two B-17s that had not been able to drop over Wilhelmshaven dropped their bombs on Emden during the return leg.

The bombing was described as 'fair', and the AAF gunners also lodged claims for 22 fighters shot down for the loss of one Fortress (a 305th BG machine, flown by a Lt Beckham). Although the gunners' claims were typically over-exaggerated, German records indicate that seven fighters were actually destroyed intercepting this raid – the heaviest losses suffered by the *Jagdwaffe* to date.

This mission was the start of the joint RAF/AAF 'round the clock bombing' campaign that would dominate the air war in Europe from now until VE-Day.

The next German target chosen to be bombed was the rail marshalling yard at Hamm, deep in the well-defended Ruhr Valley. Again, weather hampered the efforts of the VIII BC, and the first raid was scrubbed after launching on 2 February. Two days later the bombers got as far as northwest Germany before again being forced to turn back due to poor weather. Some 86 bombers had sortied on this mission, and 39 of them hastily released their bombs on a convoy that had been spotted off the coast of Emden during the return flight.

By this stage the Fortress formation had became dangerously strung out, and the *Jagdwaffe* clinically seized its opportunity to redress its poor showing of 27 January. Five B-17s, including two from the 91st BG and two from the 305th BG, were destroyed, with one of the latter bombers being involved in a head-on collision with an Fw 190 from JG 1.

Despite having lost around a third of all scheduled missions to bad weather, a number of VIII BC crews, and their aircraft, could now boast mission tallies in double figures. One such combination was the 91st BG crew, led by Capt W J Crumm, in B-17F 41-24490 *Jack the Ripper*. Part of the 324th BS, their completion of the unsuccessful Hamm raid on 4 February had taken their tally to 11, and they were duly selected by the Eighth Air Force to return to the USA to help write the handbook for combat crews destined for the ETO. This would subsequently prove to be the 'bible' for all aircrew assigned to Fortress groups within VIII BC.

More bad weather grounded the 'Forts' until 14 February, when VIII BC again flew an abortive strike on Hamm. Two days later 71 B-17s and 18 B-24s were despatched to 'Flak City' (St Nazaire) for the first time since the costly raid on 3 January, and although the weather was good over the target, most of the bombardiers missed the aiming point of the

Ball turret gunner S/Sgt Maynard H 'Snuffy' Smith of the 423rd BS/306th BG was the first enlisted man in the Eighth Air Force to receive the Medal of Honor. The award was made for his actions on the mission to St Nazaire on May Day 1943

U-boat basin locks. Despite this, the AAF proclaimed 'excellent' results for the raid.

The 14 February mission had seen I./JG 2 and 9./JG 26 live up to their reputation as the most dangerous fighter opposition on the continent. Both units had used their innovative tactics, and experience, to down six B-17s as the formation headed north-east from St Nazaire – the 303rd, 305th and 306th BGs each lost two bombers apiece.

Sent to Germany for a third time on 26 February, VIII BC again had to abort the briefed attack on its primary target of Bremen due to a heavy undercast. The secondary target was the port facility at Wilhelmshaven, and around 150 tons of bombs were dropped in a scattered pattern. The *Jagdwaffe* was present in abundance, with the first attacks taking place about 30 miles from the coast. The crews of the single- and twin-engined fighters were so determined in their mission that they kept up their attacks all the way to the target. Aside from the now standard head-on passes, the fighters also used aerial bombing against the tightly-packed formations. Finally, several crews also reported seeing parachute mines fired from guns on the ground, this new weapon having never previously been encountered. The combination of co-ordinated attacks by fighters and deadly flak resulted in seven 1st BW Fortresses being destroyed – four of these came from the 305th BG and two from the 91st BG.

February had proved to be particularly hard on VIII BC, the command losing 22 bombers during the four raids permitted by weather. And more of the same occurred in March.

A four-group effort was despatched to strike at Hamm on the 4th, but as with the previous attempts to bomb this target, weather had the whip hand. Two of the groups (303rd and 305th BGs) diverted south to Rotterdam when a thick sea haze reduced visibility over the North Sea to less than 1000 yards, whilst the 306th BG returned to Thurleigh without having dropped a single bomb. As per SOP, strict radio silence had been maintained throughout the mission, leaving the 16 crews from the 91st BG totally unaware that their compatriots had turned back.

Indeed, formation leader, 22-year-old Maj Paul Fishburne, only realised he and his men were on their own when the cloud cleared near to the German coastline. Choosing to press on, the 91st BG got to within half-an-hour of their target before the first fighters arrived. Despite the attention of the *Jagdwaffe*, and an intense flak barrage over Hamm itself, the group performed a textbook attack on the rail marshalling yard that saw its bombs hit the briefed MPI.

The fighter attacks during the bombing run itself had been sporadic and uncoordinated, but that all changed once the 91st had turned westward for home. With the full weight of the Luftwaffe's defence system thrown up against them, the beleaguered Fortress gunners fended off the fighters for over an hour. The sheer ferocity of these attacks is well relayed by the 323rd BS's Lt Charles Giauque, who was at the controls of B-17F 41-24524 *The EAGLE'S WRATH*;

'After heading for home, we initially met with no resistance at all, but that didn't last. Just before the Dutch border the fighters came, and we estimated that there were at least 175 of them during the balance of the fight prior to reaching the Channel. They were mostly Fw 190s and Bf 110s. The latter type had never given us a problem before, but on this mission they were as aggressive as the '190s. The attacks were from all positions of the clock, and from low to high.'

Another participant in this legendary action was Lt William D Beasley, who reported during the mission debrief at Bassingbourn that he had never seen so many enemy fighters, and that his bomber (struggling along with *three* faulty engines!) had suffered simultaneous attacks from four different types of German fighters.

Four B-17s were lost by the 91st BG on the Hamm raid, three of which fell to the Fw 190s of II./JG 1. The first of these crashed near to the target area, B-17F 42-5370 of the 324th BS (flown by Lt Harold H Henderson) spinning out of formation on fire north-west of Münster. There were no

B-17F-25-BO 41-24577 *HELL'S ANGELS* of the 358th BS/303rd BG was the first heavy bomber to complete an Eighth Air Force tour of 25 missions, between 16 October 1942 and 14 May 1943. After flying 48 missions, all without an abort, 41-24577 was flown back to the USA on 10 February 1944, having been autographed by hundreds of members of the 303rd BG at Molesworth. Once back home, it joined up with its original pilot, Capt Irl Baldwin, for a War Bond tour of industrial war plants. ***HELL'S ANGELS*** was broken up for scrap at Searcey Field, in Stillwater, Oklahoma, in August 1945 (*USAF*)

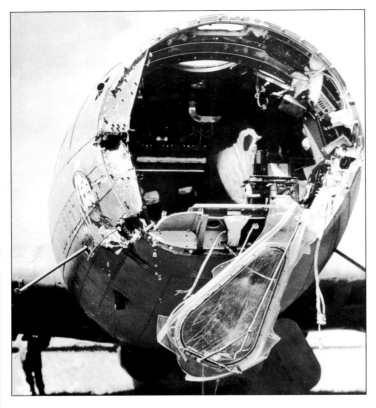

B-17F-65-BO 42-29673 *OLD BILL* of the 365th BS/305th BG is seen in the aftermath of the raid of 15 May 1943. Its pilot, 1Lt William Whitson, helped by gunner Albert Haymon and bombardier 1Lt Robert W Barrall, nursed this aircraft back to Chelveston after it had been riddled with 20 mm cannon fire from fighters over Heligoland. The Plexiglas nose had been shot out in the action, killing navigator 2Lt Douglas Van Able, and injuring Barrall. Whitson and Barrall were each awarded the DSC, whilst the rest of the 11-man crew (which included a photographer) received eight Silver Stars and seven Purple Hearts. 'Old Bill' was the creation of British artist and *Stars and Stripes* cartoonist Bruce Bairnsfather, who adorned the nose of the aircraft with his rendition of a World War 1 soldier (*via* Bill Donald)

survivors. The substantial damage suffered by many of the bombers during the hour-long aerial assault by the *Jagdwaffe* sealed the fate of the next two to fall. Three crippled Fortresses had been forced to drop out of the main formation with shot-out engines, and this trio in turn formed a tight defensive vic in an effort to fend off their attackers. This worked for a while until B-17F 41-24549 *Stupen-Taket*, flown by the 323rd BS's Capt Martin W McCarty, was lost when an Fw 190 attacked it from the three o'clock position. Only the bombardier and ball turret gunner survived.

Minutes later Lt Ralph A Felton's B-17F 41-24512 *Rose O'Day* (from the 322nd BS) succumbed to an accurate burst of fire from a Bf 110 – three crewmen parachuted into captivity. The last bomber lost was B-17F 41-24464 *Excalibur*, which made it as far as the North Sea before its pilot, Lt Allen Brill of the 324th BS, was forced to ditch. The ball turret gunner was swept away in the freezing – and choppy – water soon after the bomber was evacuated, and the pilot, and his co-pilot, Lt Allen W Lowry, were lost whilst ensuring the safe escape of the remaining seven crewmen. Both were later awarded posthumous Distinguished Service Crosses for their bravery, whilst the 91st BG received the first Distinguished Unit Citation (DUC) given to an VIII BC group for its remarkable efforts on 4 March. This latter award was not conferred until 1947, however!

Another marshalling yard, this time at Rennes, in the Brittany region of France, provided the target for the next major VIII BC attack flown on 8 March. A total of 54 B-17s were despatched, with Brig Gen Hayward Hansell flying with a crew from the 305th BG. Only four bombers aborted, and the Fortresses duly 'plastered' the marshalling yards from end to end, effectively stopping any supplies reaching German bases in Brittany for up to four days. Over the next five days two more marshalling yards in France were bombed without loss to the attackers.

On 18 March Eaker ordered a maximum effort to bomb the Bremer Vulkan Schiffbau shipbuilding yards at Vegesack, which had escaped attack on 27 January due to poor weather. This time conditions were perfect, and 73 Fortresses and 24 Liberators – the highest number of 'heavies' yet sent to Germany – were assembled for the raid. Fighters were first encountered near Heligoland, and during the bomb run the leading 303rd BG formation of 22 aircraft bore the brunt of most of the attacks.

Also, accurate flak bracketed the 303rd's B-17s, with the 359th BS (the lowest squadron in the formation) being particularly badly hit. The unit was being led by Capt Harold Stouse in B-17F 41-24561 *THE DUCHESS*, and at 24,000 ft, with less than a minute to go before over-flying the bomb release point, lead bombardier 1Lt Jack W Mathis had his eye firmly fixed to the Norden bombsight. Seconds later a shell deto-nated near to the right side of the B-17 nose, shattering part of the bomber's Plexiglas nose and flinging the bombardier to the back of his compartment, some nine feet behind him.

The flying shrapnel had inflicted mortal wounds on Mathis – his right arm had been all but severed above the elbow and his side and abdomen had been badly punctured – but he still managed to drag himself back to his bombsight to release his bombs exactly on time. This was crucial, for Mathis was performing the bomb-aiming for the entire 359th BS. The navigator, who had also been knocked off his feet by the explosion, only realised the seriousness of the bombardier's injuries when he collapsed over his bombsight whilst attempting to reach the switch that closed the bomb-bay doors.

THE DUCHESS made it safely back to Molesworth, where the last few moments of Jack Mathis's life were relayed by the navigator. His actions resulted in the 359th achieving a highly accurate bombing pattern, and saw him posthumously awarded his country's highest military decora-tion, the Medal of Honor, for 'conspicuous gallantry and intrepidity above and beyond the call of duty'.

The pin-point bombing of the 359th BS reflected the results achieved by the rest of the force that day. Vegesack was officially described as hav-ing been 'extremely heavily damaged' by the 268 tons of high-explosive. Indeed, the 305th BG was deemed to have placed 76 per cent of its bombs within 1000 ft of the MPI.

For the loss of two bombers (including a B-17 from the 303rd BG), the 'heavies' had severely damaged seven U-boats and destroyed two-thirds of the shipyard, and its machinery plant – destruction revealed by photo-graphic reconnaissance conducted in the wake of the mission. British Prime Minister Winston Churchill and the RAF's Chief of Air Staff, Air Marshal Sir Charles Portal, recognised the importance of the success achieved on this raid, and they both sent congratulatory messages to Gen Eaker.

Sadly, the next three missions – to Wilhelmshaven, Rouen and Rotter-dam – did not go quite as well, and eight bombers were lost. On the last of these, flown on 31 March, the E-boat pens in the Dutch port were

YB-40 gunships (in this instance the variant prototype, XB-40 41-24341, which was converted by Vega at Burbank, California, in November 1942 from a standard B-17F-1-BO) made their operational debut on 29 May 1943 when seven aircraft from the 92nd BG took part in their first mission. Intended to provide extra firepower for the beleaguered bomber formations, the YB-40s, which weighed almost five tons more than the standard B-17, proved less than successful as multi-gunned destroyer-escorts. Losses were not made good, although the YB-40s continued flying missions until the end of July 1943 (*Boeing*)

missed completely due to cloud cover, and 300 Dutch civilians were either killed or wounded.

On 4 April Eaker switched back to targets in France, sending a large force to bomb the vast Renault factory in the Billancourt district of south-eastern Paris. It took two hours for the four B-17 groups despatched to complete assembly, 97 Fortresses eventually departing the skies of Bedfordshire for the rendezvous point over Beachy Head. However, by the time landfall was made at Dieppe only 85 B-17s remained, 12 having aborted through malfunctions. Escorting Spitfires stayed with the penetrating force virtually all the way to the target, deterring any attacks by the Luftwaffe. At 1414 hours the bombers reached their target, and 251 tons of HE rained down on Paris.

Flak was moderate and not too accurate, and despite industrial haze blanketing much of the city itself, crews were able to clearly pick out the Renault works. Most of the 81 tons that struck 19 factory buildings was dropped by the 18 B-17s of the leading 305th BG formation, headed by Maj Thomas K McGhee in *We The People*, flown by Capt Cliff Pyle. Before the final group had left the target area, the entire factory, and its surrounding area, was blotted out by a thick pall of smoke that spiralled up to 4000 ft. That same smoke greatly affected the accuracy of the groups to the rear of the formation, causing many bombs to fall well outside the target area, killing a number of civilians.

Despite these regrettable casualties, the raid was deemed to have been a success, for it took the Germans six months to restore the plant to full production – during which time the Wehrmacht was denied an estimated 3075 lorries.

Having been conspicuous by their absence during the penetration and bombing phases of the mission, German fighters finally appeared some five minutes after the last bombs had struck the target. Between 50 and 75 Fw 190s from I./JG 2 and the operational *Staffel* of training unit JG 105 pressed home their attacks all the way to Rouen, where the Fw 190s and Bf 109s of II. and III./JG 26 took up the chase. Four B-17s were downed during a series of frontal attacks, sometimes by four and six fighters at a time, until the Spitfire escort reappeared to provide withdrawal support.

To take full effect of the chaos caused by a head-on interception from eleven, twelve, or one o'clock high, the *Jagdwaffe* was now instructing its attacking *Schwärme* to group their passes as closely together as they dared. That meant the distance between attacking waves could be as small as 1000 to 1500 yards, leaving the bombers with little time to perform defensive manoeuvres.

The Germans did not have it all their own way on the 4th however, as the AAF gunners claimed 47 fighters destroyed. Ten of these were credited to the gunners aboard 364th BS/305th BG B-17F *Dry Martini 4th*, piloted by Capt Allen Martini. This tally represented half of the group's claims for the mission, and set the record score for a bomber crew on a single mission. German records reveal that just two Fw 190s and a Bf 109 had actually been downed, and several other fighters damaged, during the entire engagement.

The very next day the ERLA aircraft repair works in the Belgian city of Mortsel, near Antwerp, was bombed for the very first time. A mixed force of 104 bombers was led by the 306th BG, *(text continues on page 49)*

COLOUR PLATES

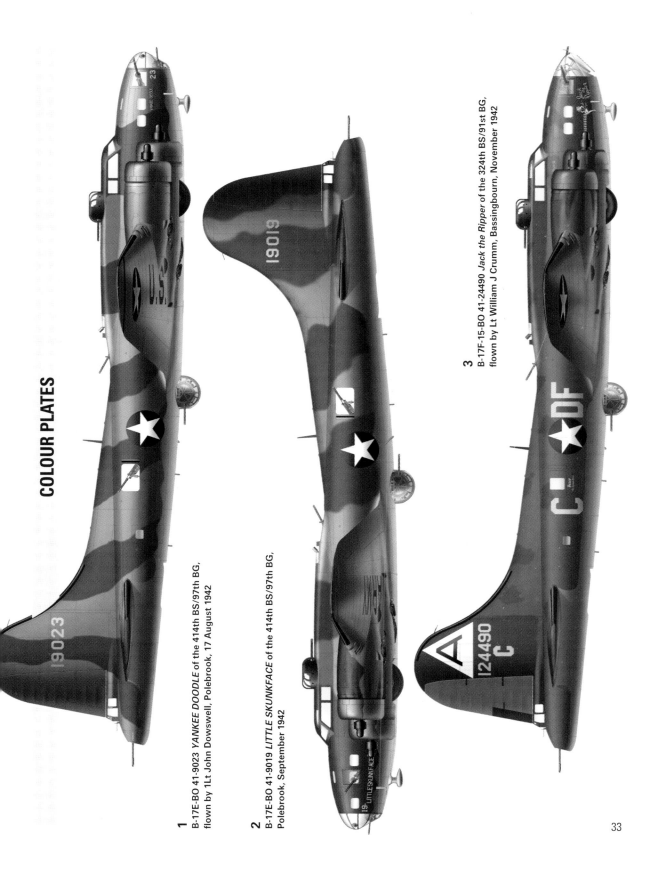

1
B-17E-BO 41-9023 *YANKEE DOODLE* of the 414th BS/97th BG,
flown by 1Lt John Dowswell, Polebrook, 17 August 1942

2
B-17E-BO 41-9019 *LITTLE SKUNKFACE* of the 414th BS/97th BG,
Polebrook, September 1942

3
B-17F-15-BO 41-24490 *Jack the Ripper* of the 324th BS/91st BG,
flown by Lt William J Crumm, Bassingbourn, November 1942

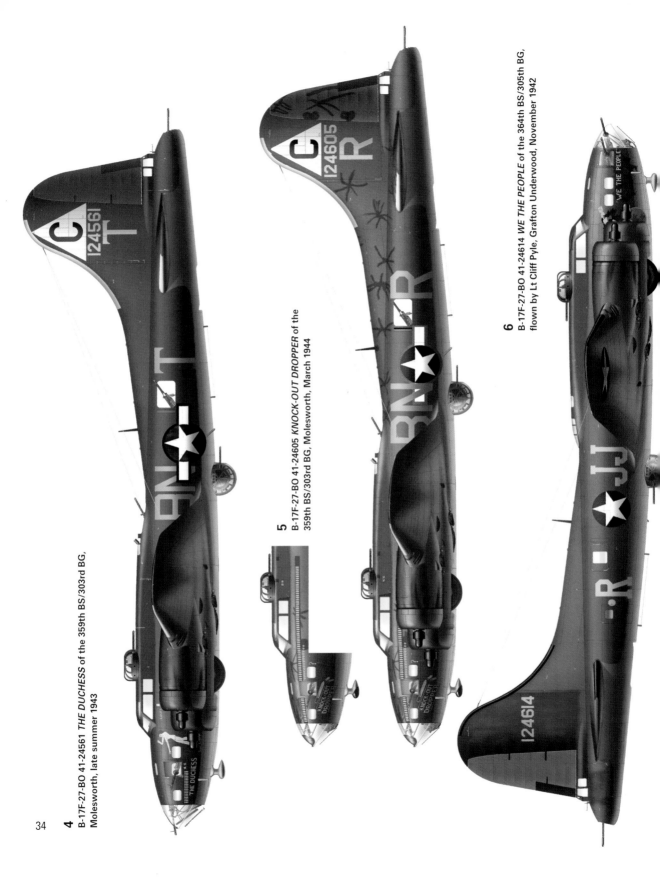

34

4
B-17F-27-BO 41-24561 *THE DUCHESS* of the 359th BS/303rd BG,
Molesworth, late summer 1943

5
B-17F-27-BO 41-24605 *KNOCK-OUT DROPPER* of the
359th BS/303rd BG, Molesworth, March 1944

6
B-17F-27-BO 41-24614 *WE THE PEOPLE* of the 364th BS/305th BG,
flown by Lt Cliff Pyle, Grafton Underwood, November 1942

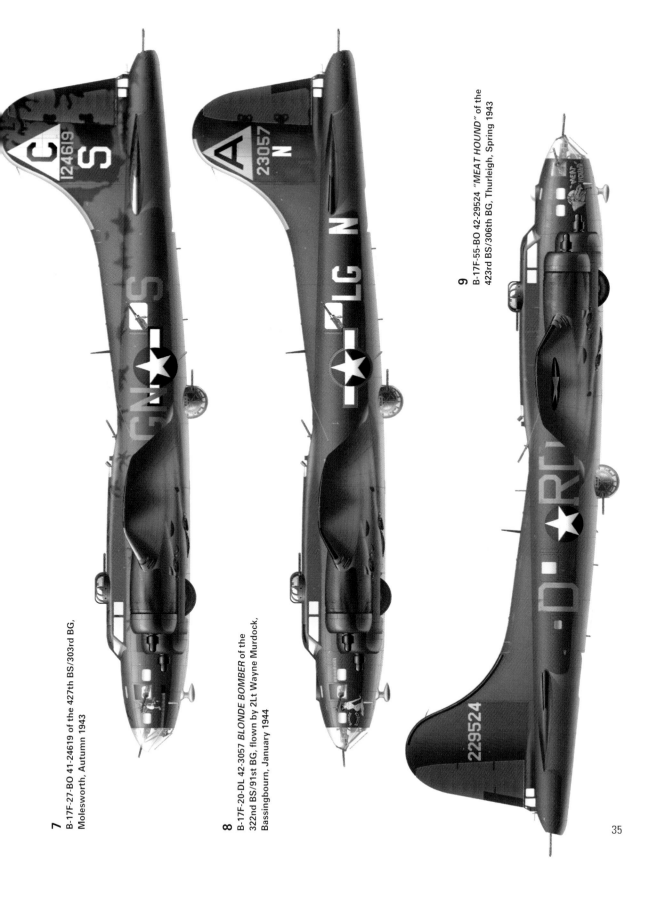

7
B-17F-27-BO 41-24619 of the 427th BS/303rd BG,
Molesworth, Autumn 1943

8
B-17F-20-DL 42-3057 *BLONDE BOMBER* of the
322nd BS/91st BG, flown by 2Lt Wayne Murdock,
Bassingbourn, January 1944

9
B-17F-55-BO 42-29524 *"MEAT HOUND"* of the
423rd BS/306th BG, Thurleigh, Spring 1943

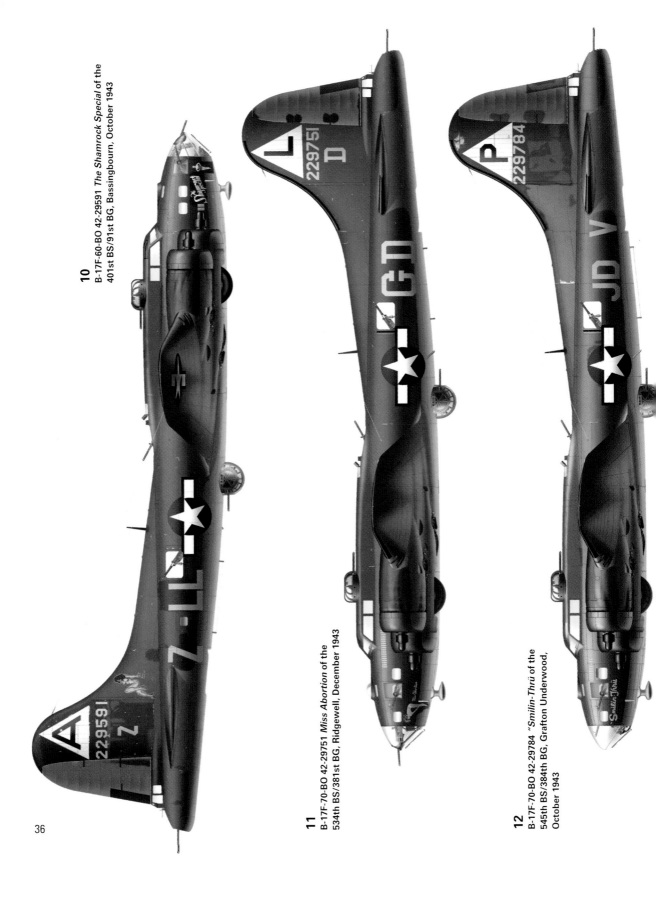

10
B-17F-60-BO 42-29591 *The Shamrock Special* of the
401st BS/91st BG, Bassingbourn, October 1943

11
B-17F-70-BO 42-29751 *Miss Abortion* of the
534th BS/381st BG, Ridgewell, December 1943

12
B-17F-70-BO 42-29784 *"Smilin-Thru"* of the
545th BS/384th BG, Grafton Underwood,
October 1943

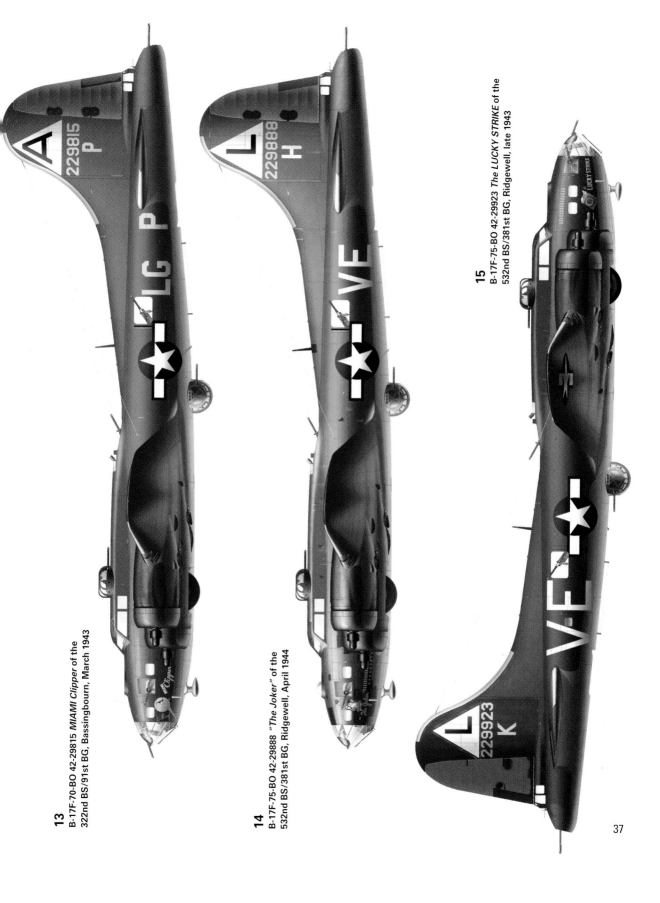

13
B-17F-70-BO 42-29815 *MIAMI Clipper* of the
322nd BS/91st BG, Bassingbourn, March 1943

14
B-17F-75-BO 42-29888 *"The Joker"* of the
532nd BS/381st BG, Ridgewell, April 1944

15
B-17F-75-BO 42-29923 *The LUCKY STRIKE* of the
532nd BS/381st BG, Ridgewell, late 1943

16
B-17F-80-BO 42-29947 *WABASH CANNONBALL* of the
322nd BS/91st BG at Bassingbourn, early 1944

17
B-17F-80-BO 42-29953 *Wolfess* of the
364th BS/305th BG, Chelveston,
November 1943

18
B-17F-115-BO 42-30712 *MISS MINOOKIE* of the
323rd BS/91st BG, Bassingbourn, September 1943

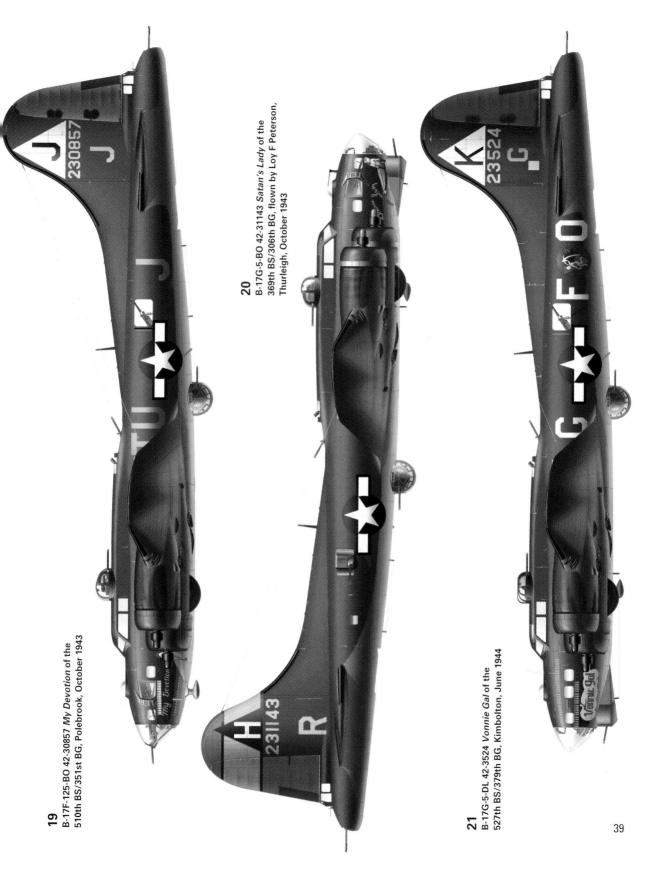

19
B-17F-125-BO 42-30857 *My Devotion* of the
510th BS/351st BG, Polebrook, October 1943

20
B-17G-5-BO 42-31143 *Satan's Lady* of the
369th BS/306th BG, flown by Loy F Peterson,
Thurleigh, October 1943

21
B-17G-5-DL 42-3524 *Vonnie Gal* of the
527th BS/379th BG, Kimbolton, June 1944

22
B-17G-15-BO 42-31353 *QUEENIE* of the
322nd BS/91st BG, flown by Lt Bob
Fancher, Bassingbourn, March 1944

23
B-17G-15-BO 42-31367 *Chow-hound* of the
322nd BS/91st BG, flown by 1Lt Jerold
Newquist, Bassingbourn, April 1944

24
B-17G-20-BO 42-31585 *MOUNT 'N RIDE* of the
323rd BS/91st BG, flown by Lt Roman Maziarz,
Bassingbourn, February 1944

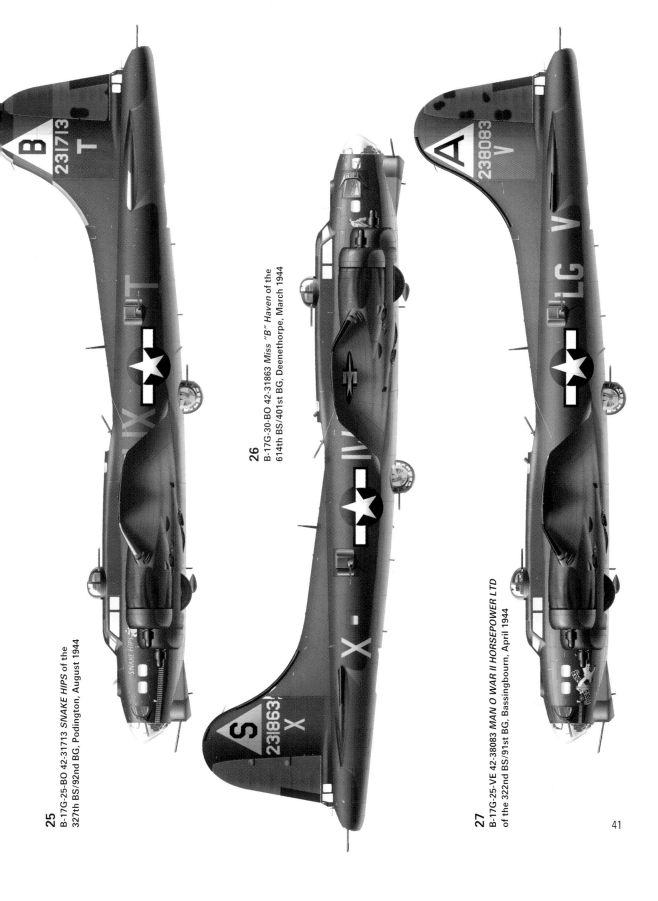

25
B-17G-25-BO 42-31713 *SNAKE HIPS* of the
327th BS/92nd BG, Podington, August 1944

26
B-17G-30-BO 42-31863 *Miss "B" Haven* of the
614th BS/401st BG, Deenethorpe, March 1944

27
B-17G-25-VE 42-38083 *MAN O WAR II HORSEPOWER LTD*
of the 322nd BS/91st BG, Bassingbourn, April 1944

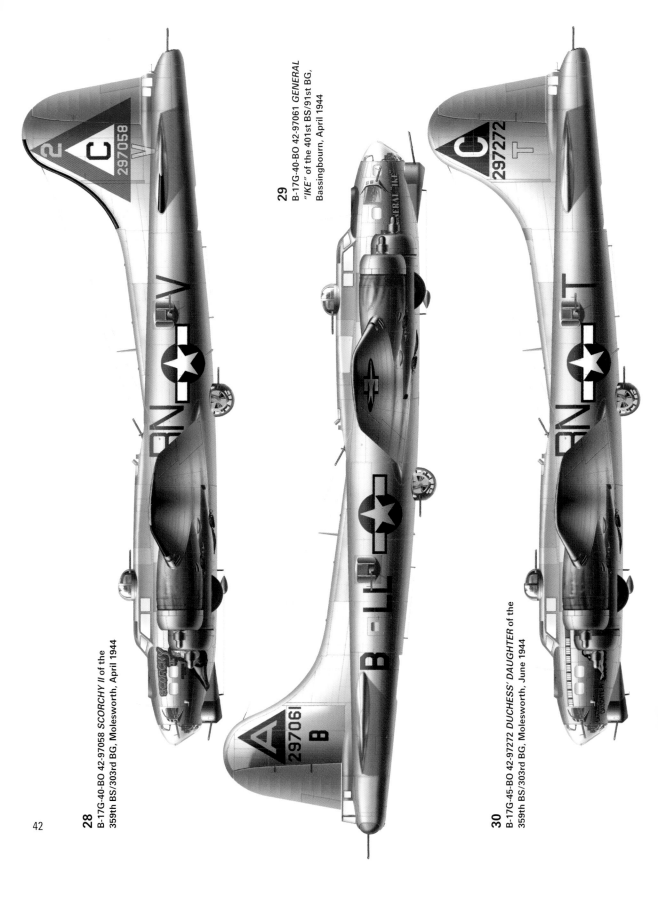

28
B-17G-40-BO 42-97058 *SCORCHY II* of the
359th BS/303rd BG, Molesworth, April 1944

29
B-17G-40-BO 42-97061 *GENERAL
"IKE"* of the 401st BS/91st BG,
Bassingbourn, April 1944

30
B-17G-45-BO 42-97272 *DUCHESS' DAUGHTER* of the
359th BS/303rd BG, Molesworth, June 1944

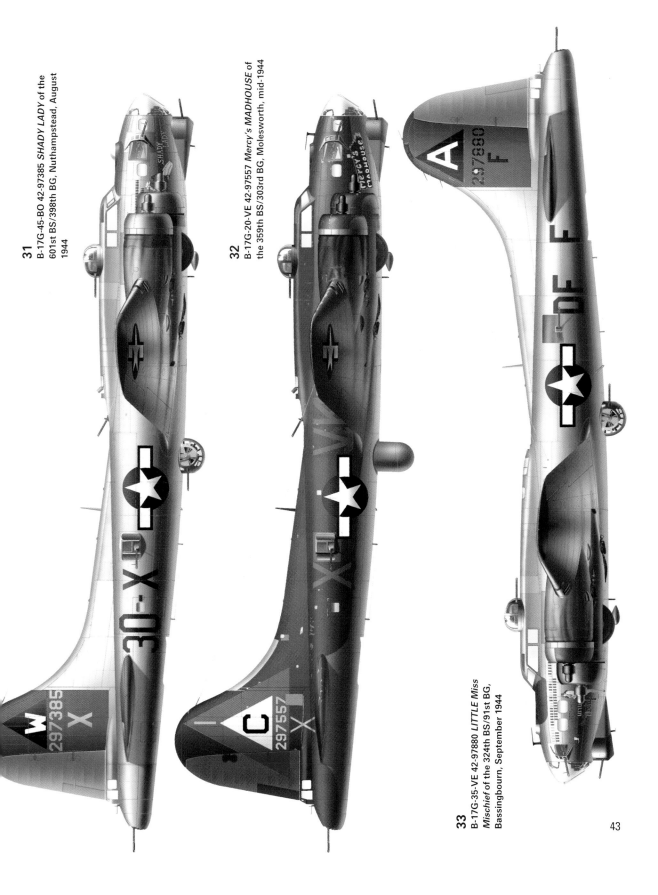

31
B-17G-45-BO 42-97385 *SHADY LADY* of the
601st BS/398th BG, Nuthampstead, August
1944

32
B-17G-20-VE 42-97557 *Mercy's MADHOUSE* of
the 359th BS/303rd BG, Molesworth, mid-1944

33
B-17G-35-VE 42-97880 *LITTLE Miss
Mischief* of the 324th BS/91st BG,
Bassingbourn, September 1944

43

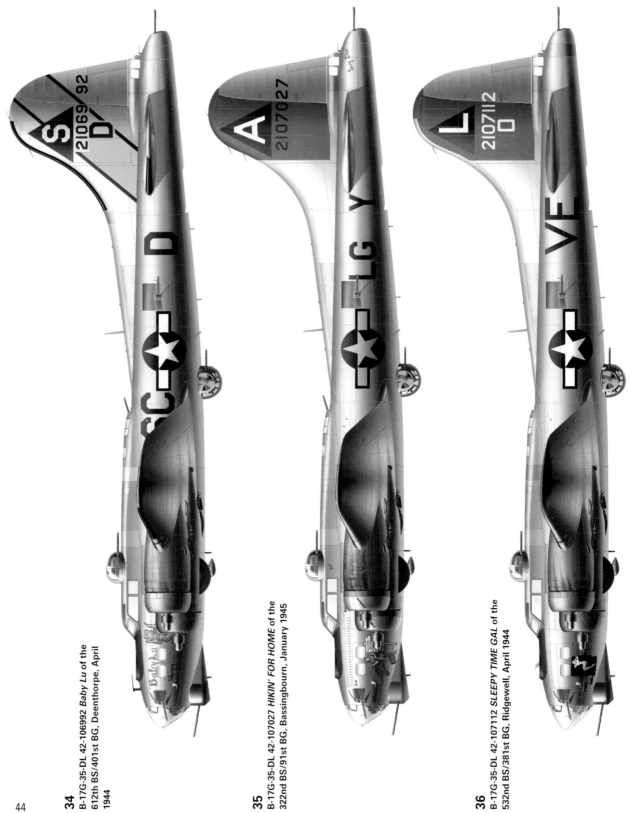

34
B-17G-35-DL 42-106992 *Baby Lu* of the
612th BS/401st BG, Deenthorpe, April
1944

35
B-17G-35-DL 42-107027 *HIKIN' FOR HOME* of the
322nd BS/91st BG, Bassingbourn, January 1945

36
B-17G-35-DL 42-107112 *SLEEPY TIME GAL* of the
532nd BS/381st BG, Ridgewell, April 1944

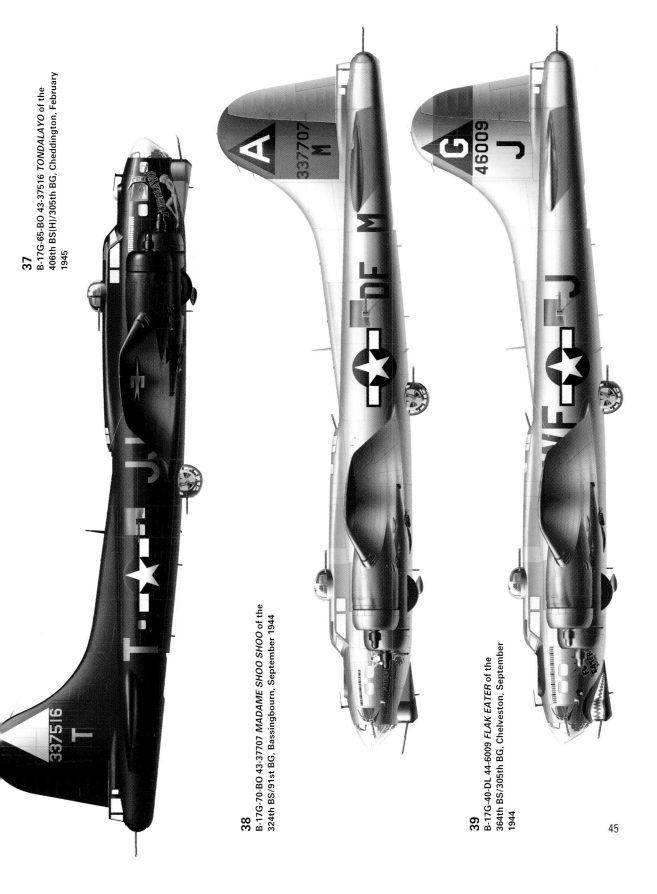

37
B-17G-65-BO 43-37516 *TONDALAYO* of the
406th BS(H)/305th BG, Cheddington, February
1945

38
B-17G-70-BO 43-37707 *MADAME SHOO SHOO* of the
324th BS/91st BG, Bassingbourn, September 1944

39
B-17G-40-DL 44-6009 *FLAK EATER* of the
364th BS/305th BG, Chelveston, September
1944

This nose-art section has been specially created by profile artist Mark Styling so as to better illustrate the colourful artworks worn by the Flying Fortresses featured in profile. These drawings have been produced following exhaustive cross-referencing with published bomb group histories, correspondence with surviving veterans and the detailed study of original photographs.

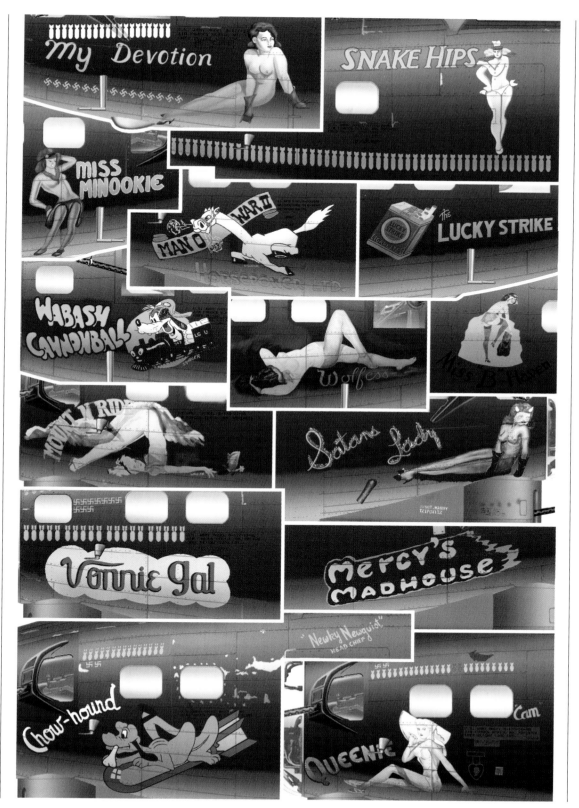

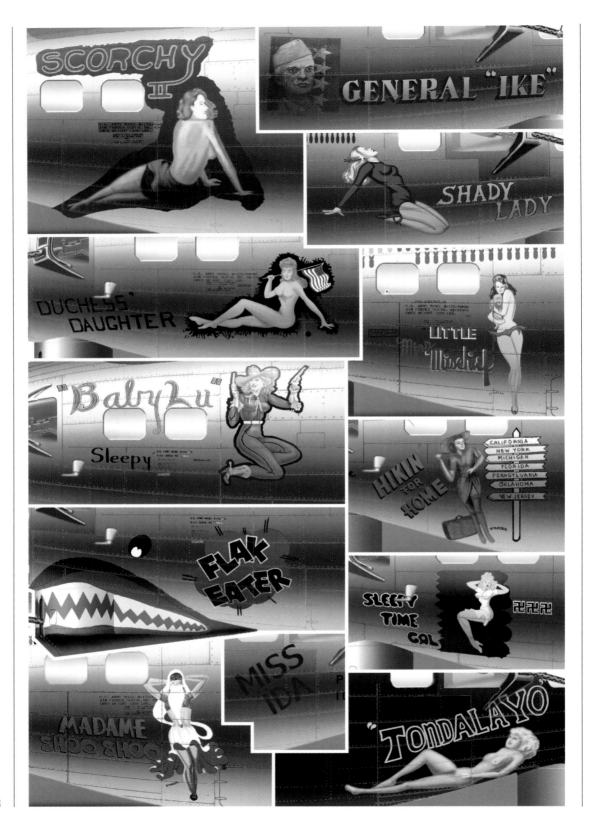

which had not suffered the loss of a B-17 during its previous six missions. The 'heavies' were intercepted by III./JG 26 prior to reaching the target, and despite the presence of fighter escorts, which were again positioned too far above and behind to prevent the attack, the Fw 190 pilots quickly put an end to the 306th's recent mission record. Splitting up its formation with their first pass, the fighters went after flak-damaged B-17F *Lil Abner*, flown by Lt Clarence Fisher. The bomber was finished off by JG 26's *Geschwaderkommodore*, Maj 'Pips' Priller, taking his score to 84 kills.

During this same opening head-on attack, Priller's successor as III.*Gruppe Kommandeur*, Hauptmann Friedrich 'Fritz' Geisshardt, was struck in the abdomen by return fire, and although he succeeded in performing a wheels-up landing at St Denis-Westrem, he died from loss of blood in Ghent hospital the next morning. Decorated with the knight's cross and oakleaves, and having scored 102 confirmed kills during service on the Eastern Front and in North Africa, Geisshardt was the first major loss inflicted on JG 26 by AAF gunners. He would not be the last.

With its bombers now dangerously out of formation, the 306th BG overshot the target and dropped its bombs on the city of Mortsel, killing 936 Belgian civilians and injuring 1342 – only four bombs actually hit the ERLA factory. Just as the group pulled away from the 'target', II./JG 26 carried out its first attack of the afternoon, in unison with I./JG 1. Three B-17s succumbed to the incessant attacks over the next ten minutes. The Fortress flown by Lt Kelly Ross was claimed by II./JG 26's *Gruppenkommandeur*, Major Wilhelm-Ferdinand 'Wutz' Galland, as his 38th victory. Fellow II.*Gruppe* ace Oberfeldwebel Adolf 'Addi' Glunz downed 1Lt William Parker's B-17 to score his 32nd kill, and Lt Robert Steelos'

Capt Robert K Morgan and the crew of B-17F-10-BO 41-24485 *"MEMPHIS BELLE"* from the 324th BS/91st BG bid farewell to Gens Devers and Eaker at Bassingbourn on 13 June 1943 before flying home to begin a Bond Tour of the USA. The crew flew their 25th, and final, mission of their tour on 17 May 1943 to Lorient. The *'BELLE* featured in a 1943 documentary about Eighth Air Force operations, made principally for American cinema audiences by Maj William Wyler, the famous Hollywood director (*USAF*)

Fortress fell to Oberleutnant Otto 'Stotto' Stammberger. With this victory, the latter pilot's tally now reached five.

A further 13 bombers returned to England with varying degrees of damage, including one carrying newly-promoted Brig Gen Frank Armstrong, who had been given command of the 1st Combat Bombardment Wing (CBW) just days earlier. He was flying as an observer in a 306th BG Fortress that was badly mauled by cannon fire, although the skill of its pilot, Group Executive Maj James Wilson, brought the bomber safely home to Thurleigh.

BREMEN RAID

Poor weather saw no further large raids sent to the continent until 17 April, when crews throughout eastern England were sent to bomb the Focke-Wulf plant at Bremen – a record 115 B-17s were assembled. For the first time VIII BC was able to despatch two large-scale combat wings to Germany, the 91st and 306th BGs comprising the first wing, and the 303rd and 305th BGs making up the second. Each wing formation consisted of three group boxes of 18-21 aircraft, flown closely together for mutual firepower and protection.

Eight bombers returned to England early with malfunctions, leaving the remaining 107 B-17s to continue across the North Sea. The formation had been detected by enemy reconnaissance aircraft a full hour before they came in sight of the German coast, and the Luftwaffe fighter controllers delayed the interception until the 'heavies' had commenced their bombing run. This allowed the 496 flak batteries around Bremen to open up with a box barrage, and their fire decimated the 401st BS/91st BG, whose six aircraft were flying in the hated low squadron position of the leading group. Dubbed 'Purple Heart Corner', the low squadron slot was also the most vulnerable to attack both by flak and fighters, as the losses to the 401st graphically proved.

All six of its B-17s went down, five falling to flak and a sixth to Fw 190s from either III./JG 54 or JG 11 – 27 crewman escaped their crashing aircraft to become PoWs.

The first fighters had engaged the leading formations (the 91st and 306th BGs) as the bombers flew over the Friesian Isles, north-west of Bremen, and they had soon inflicted grievous damage on a number of Fortresses in the leading wing. Seemingly unconcerned by the flak barrage that was still bursting in amongst the bombers, the *Jagdwaffe* continued to launch wave after wave of Fw 190s in a seemingly endless series of head-on attacks. Their tenacity paid off, for the 306th lost no less than ten B-17s on the mission. A further 48 Fortresses also received damage to varying degrees, including yet another 306th BG aircraft which came home with a parachute harness tied to control cables that had been shot away by cannon fire.

The destruction of 16 B-17s on this raid represented a 50 per cent rise in the loss rate previously suffered by VIII BC on a single mission, and this grim statistic was only partially offset by the results of the bombing. It was estimated that a fair percentage of the 531 1000-lb bombs dropped on the Focke Wulf Flugzeugbau had hit the target, because half of the factory was destroyed. However, it was later learned that construction of fighters at the site had been halted six months earlier by Albert Speer, German

Hollywood movie star Capt Clark Gable was photographed after returning from a 303rd BG mission to Antwerp on 4 May 1943 in 359th BS B-17F-27-BO 41-24635 *The 8 Ball Mk II*. In October 1942 Gable had graduated from the Officers' Candidate School in Miami as a second lieutenant, and attended aerial gunnery school until February 1943. On the personal insistence of Gen 'Hap' Arnold, Chief of the American Air Staff, he was assigned to the 351st BG to make a motion picture of gunners in action. Gable flew a handful of combat missions and completed some footage for the film, *Combat America*. *The 8 Ball Mk II* survived the war also, finishing its days at Albuquerque, New Mexico, in 1945
(*Harry D Gobrecht via Brian McGuire*)

armaments minister, as part of his fighter production dispersal plan.

Bomber gunners put in claims for 63 fighters destroyed, but in reality only ten German aircraft had actually been shot down – most of the parachutes crews saw during the two-hour battle above Bremen had belonged to American airmen.

VIII BC crews received a boost to their flagging morale with the arrival of four new B-17 groups (the 94th, 95th, 96th and 351st BGs, although only the latter outfit was assigned to the 1st CBW) that had been promised to the Eighth Air Force following the Casablanca Conference in mid-February. Despite the increasing losses, VIII BC's results from raids on German targets in particular, had convinced senior Allied commanders that Gen Eaker's daylight bombing strategy could work.

While the new groups continued training, Gen Eaker scheduled another attack on St Nazaire for May Day. Thick cloud over the target curtailed bombing attempts, and due to a navigational error, the 306th BG formation strayed closer to the French coast than they had been briefed. When land was spotted through the cloud below, the lead navigator mistook the Brest Peninsular for Land's End and started to descend for landing. The formation was immediately bracketed by an accurate flak barrage and six aircraft were shot down, whilst a seventh fell to fighters from JG 2. Many others were damaged by shrapnel.

Amongst the latter was 423rd BS B-17F 42-29649, flown by 1Lt Lewis P Johnson. Indeed, it only made it back to England thanks to the astounding efforts of ball gunner S/Sgt Maynard 'Snuffy' Smith, who was flying his first mission. The bomber was struck several times by flak, which caused fires to break out in the radio compartment and tail section. His ball turret knocked out, Smith crawled into the fuselage of the burning bomber in time to see the waist gunners and radio operators – all veterans of previous missions – bale out. He chose to stay, fighting the blaze with a hand-held extinguisher. Cut off from the crew in the front of the B-17 by the radio compartment fire, Smith assumed that they too were staying put as the bomber remained in formation.

Having all but doused out the fire in the rear of the aircraft, he then discovered the badly wounded tail gunner collapsed outside his compartment. After treating his wounds as best he could, Smith returned to fight the radio room blaze, which was being fuelled by escaping oxygen bottles. In between fighting the fire and tending the tail gunner, Smith also shot off a few rounds from the waist guns at several Fw 190s that had attacked the formation! He then dragged ammunition boxes away from the centre of the blaze and threw them out of a gaping hole in the fuselage.

Smith battled the blaze for a full 90 minutes, and after using the last of the extinguishers, he attempted to smother the fire with clothing – he even resorted to urinating on the flames. The blaze had been so intense that part of the bomber's structure had physically melted, and the pilot had to gingerly let down at Predannack, near Land's End. Having suffered irreparable damage, including a gaping hole where the fire had burnt through the side of the radio room, 42-29649 was reduced to scrap on the spot.

Several weeks later, Maynard 'Snuffy' Smith became the first enlisted man in the Eighth Air Force to receive the Medal of Honor for his actions on this mission.

Three days after 'Snuffy' Smith's epic mission, on 4 May, Gen Eaker sent 79 B-17s on a five-hour round trip to the Ford and General Motors plant at Antwerp. In a first for the Eighth Air Force, the bombers' escort of 12 Allied fighter squadrons included six units equipped with P-47 Thunderbolts (see *Osprey Aircraft of the Aces 24 - Thunderbolt Aces of the Eighth Air Force* for further details). Novices at escorting bombers, the 4th and 56th FGs were positioned too high above the B-17s to intercept the attacking German fighters, but the close

escort wings – Spitfires from Biggin Hill and Northolt – used their combat experience to good effect by keeping the attacking Fw 190s from JG 26 at bay. As a result, not a single B-17 was lost, and the *Geschwader* was severely chastised by Reichsmarschall Herman Göring, who labelled the pilots 'cowardly dogs'.

May 1943 was a month of many changes for the Eighth Air Force, and the 92nd BG in particular. In January 1943 Maj Robert B Keck had left the group for the USA in order to train a flight equipped with the new, and secret, YB-40. Having completed its crew training role, the 92nd BG was being returned to combat operations at Alconbury, and one of it first tasks would be to evaluate the 'multi-gunned' YB-40. No less than 16 machine guns (and an extra top turret), fed by 12,400 rounds, were fitted in this aircraft, which was intended as a 'destroyer escort' for conventional Fortresses. Thirteen YB-40s were assigned to the 327th BS, and Maj Keck became its CO. Their arrival on 8 May heralded the resumption of combat missions for the 92nd BG.

Six days later, the Polebrook-based 351st BG participated in its first raid on Germany, allowing Gen Eaker to despatch more than 200 B-17s and B-24s. Numerous feint attacks were made on various targets across western Europe in an attempt to mask the true destination of the force, but the German fighter controllers swiftly reacted once they realised that

A 366th BS/305th BG B-17F flies over the Hüls synthetic rubber plant (then the most heavily defended target in the Reich), near Recklinghausen on the edge of the Ruhr, on 22 June 1943. By the time 183 B-17s had bombed the target, smoke from the burning plant had risen as high as 17,000 ft. Production was curtailed for a month, and full production was not resumed for five months after that. Fighters and flak brought down 16 B-17s, and another 170 bombers received damage (*USAF*)

the Germania and Deutsch Werke shipyards at Kiel were the primary targets for the unescorted bombers of the 1st BW.

Such a large number of heavy bombers had never previously been seen over Germany, although this did little to deter the attacking *Jagdflieger*. They drew first blood 20 miles off the enemy coast when 359th BS/303rd BG B-17F *F D R's Potato Peeler Kids*, flown by Capt Ross C Bales, was shot down. With Bales was Mark Mathis, whose brother Jack had been killed over Vegesack. The Kiel raid was Mark Mathis' fourth mission, and although nine 'chutes were seen to come out of the B-17, all ten crew perished in the North Sea.

Kiel was attacked at 12.05, post-mission reconnaissance deeming the bomb-aiming to have been 'good' on this occasion. During a four-hour period VIII BC had attacked four targets for the cost of 11 bombers. In reply, AAF gunners had claimed 67 fighters shot down. It is known that JG 26 lost at least three Fw 190s to the B-17s, with a similar number being claimed by the RAF Spitfire and AAF Thunderbolt escorts that had provided excellent fighter cover to the diversionary raids sent to strike at Antwerp and Coutrai.

Not all the bombing was accurate on the 14th, but for the first time the Eighth Air Force had shown that it was capable of mounting multiple attacks on a given day, weather permitting.

Hoping to build on this success, Eaker again split his forces on the 15th, sending the 1st BW to Wilhelmshaven and 59 B-17s from the newly-created 4th BW to the naval base at Emden. Thick cloud obscured the 1st BW's primary target and forced them to bomb alternative targets in Heligoland and Dune, and on Wangerooge Island. Despite Heligoland only being covered by 4/10ths cloud, defensive flak proved mercifully inaccurate. However, I./JG 2 was not so forgiving, the *Gruppe* claiming six B-17s destroyed (five were actually shot down), but at a price – four pilots were killed and a further four injured.

On 16 May VIII BC was stood down for 24 hours. The following day Eaker sent the 1st BW to Kiel and the 4th BW to Lorient. Three days later, 68 B-17s of the 1st BW again ventured to Kiel, having been briefed to bomb the turbine engine building that had been missed during the maximum effort raid on the 14th. Further north, 55 B-17s of the 4th BW simultaneously attacked U-boat pens at Flensburg, on the Danish coast.

Following this mission fog and rain cloaked East Anglia and the fens, preventing any further flights until 21 May, when the 1st BW was allocated Wilhelmshaven and the 4th BW Emden. Weather conditions hampered the groups attacking Wilhelmshaven, and they were further disrupted by constant head-on attacks by enemy fighters. The Emden force, meanwhile, also encountered heavy fighter opposition despite diversionary ruses at the coast. Altogether, 12 B-17s were lost on the two raids, with the 1st BW coming off worst with seven Fortresses shot down. Among them was *Dearly Beloved* of the 423rd BS/306th BG, flown by Lt Robert H Smith. His seven gunners had set a new VIII BC record with claims for 11 fighters destroyed on this mission. They ditched in the North Sea, and were all picked up by ASR and returned to Thurleigh.

As May wore on, a major restructuring of VIII BC saw several bomb groups moved further east into East Anglia to join the 4th BW as new groups arrived in England. One such new outfit was the 96th BG, whose former base at Grafton Underwood was taken over by the 384th BG, commanded by Col Budd J Peaslee, which flew into the Northampton-shire base on the 25 May. Five days earlier, the 379th BG, commanded by Col Maurice 'Mo' Preston, had moved into Kimbolton. Finally, on the last day of the month the 381st BG, led by Col Joe J Nazzaro, arrived at Ridgewell (Station 167), in Essex.

Another spell of bad weather in the final week of May restricted deep penetration missions and delayed the introduction of the new groups. Conditions improved sufficiently enough on the 29th to at last allow the 379th BG to 'get its feet wet' when they formed part of a massive force of 279 'heavies' (including, for the first time, seven YB-40s) from the 1st BW sent to bomb the heavily defended U-boat bases at La Pallice and St Nazaire. The 4th BW was to simultaneously perform a diversionary attack on a marshalling yard at Rennes. Heavy cloud moving across west-ern Europe almost resulted in the missions being scrubbed en route, but the weather steadily improved the further south the formation went.

St Nazaire, or 'Flak City', was always a hard target, and the inexperi-enced 379th BG paid a heavy price. Anti-aircraft fire downed two B-17s over the target, by which time the group had been fending off the atten-tions of Fw 190s for at least ten minutes. The first head-on attacks had been made just as the 379th had turned onto its bombing run at the Ini-tial Point. The German fighters then broke off as the B-17s flew through the worst of the St Nazaire flak, before recommencing their attacks as the group attempted to reform their defensive formations after coming off of the target. Two more Fortresses were lost as this point, and not a single one of the 30 crewmen shot down survived. A fourth B-17 was destroyed in England when it forced-landed in a brussel sprout patch.

On 11 June the 1st BW returned to north-west Germany. Its primary target of Bremen was obscured by heavy cloud, and they were forced to attack their secondary target at Wilhelmshaven instead. During the bomb run, the leading 303rd BG formation was bracketed by a severe flak bar-rage. One of the aircraft struck by shrapnel was the B-17 flown by the CO, Col Chuck Marion, the bomber losing two engines. Dramatically slowed by the damage, the Fortress was almost struck by several B-17s trailing in its wake. Indeed, it was only through the skill of the pilots of these aircraft, who performed a series of wild manoeuvres to avoid the impending collision, that no 303rd BG bombers hit each other. How-ever, the now scattered Fortresses were pounced on by Fw 190s – includ-ing one whose wing struck the nose of a 303rd BG B-17, causing both aircraft to crash.

Having again delayed their attacks until exactly the right moment, the *Jagdflieger* singled out the inexperienced 379th BG for more special treat-ment. Six of the group's 'Forts' fell to the fighters, taking the 379th's over-all losses to nine bombers (the total complement of a typical squadron) in just two missions.

On 13 June 102 B-17s in the 1st BW attacked the U-boat yards at Bre-men once again, while a smaller force of 72 B-17s from the 4th BW hit the submarine pens at Kiel, in northern Germany. Both raids proved unmit-igated disasters, with the bombing being generally poor, and the losses suffered by the Kiel force in particular exceeding those previously endured.

OPERATION *POINTBLANK*

Despite the increasing strength of the Eighth Air Force, the *Jagdwaffe* was still proving a formidable opponent. In an effort to curb the blood-letting of missions such as the raid on Kiel on 13 June, the Allies announced plans to mount a Combined Bomber Offensive (CBO). Known as Operation *Pointblank*, the primary objectives listed were the 'German submarine yards and bases, the remainder of the German aircraft industry, and ball bearings and oil'. Secondary objectives were 'synthetic rubber and tyres and military motor transport vehicles'. The plan concluded, 'It is emphasised that the reduction of the German fighter force is of primary importance: any delay in its prosecution will make the task progressively more difficult'.

Reacting immediately to the publication of *Pointblank*, Eaker sent a force of 235 bombers from both the 1st and 4th BWs on VIII BC's first really deep penetration of Germany on 22 June. The target was the large synthetic rubber plant at Hüls, near Recklinghausen, on the edge of the Ruhr. Run by Chemische Werke, the plant accounted for approximately 29 per cent of Germany's synthetic rubber output, and 18 per cent of its total rubber supply.

Most of the route to the target would be flown without fighter escort, so three diversionary raids were planned in an attempt to divert the *Jagdwaffe's* attention from the main attacking force, which would still have its work cut out coping with the numerous flak guns which made Hüls the most heavily defended target in the Reich at this time.

Illuminated by dawn's early light, the main force assembled over England and then flew a 'dog-leg' course over the North Sea to a point off the West Frisian Islands, where it turned south-west for the target. Unfortunately, the diversionary force aimed at the Ford and General Motors plants in Antwerp failed to materialise at this point, the 100th BG being delayed by ground mists and the 381st and 384th BGs – which were flying their maiden missions – running so far behind schedule that they missed their rendezvous with the Spitfires and Thunderbolts which were to escort them to Antwerp.

B-17F-85-BO 42-30037 of the 546th BS/384th BG, flown by 1Lt Lykes S Henderson, is inspected by German officers after being shot down on the Villacoublay mission on 26 June 1943 (*via Hans Heiri-Stapfer*)

Unescorted, the small diversionary force nevertheless pressed on to the Belgian city, where they were badly mauled by Luftwaffe fighters which had time to refuel after an earlier raid by RAF medium bombers. A series of head-on attacks succeeded in shooting down four B-17s, while three badly damaged survivors joined up and fought their way home at wave-top height across the Channel.

Meanwhile, the main force was once again proving the validity of the AAF's daylight bombing campaign. Accuracy was high right from the start, and by the time the trailing groups had completed their drops and turned 180-degrees to the left, smoke from the ruined plant was rising to 17,000 ft. The bombing was highly successful, and the Hüls plant was put out of action for a month – full production did not resume for a further five months. The cost of this success had been high, however, with 16 B-17s (including a YB-40 from the 303rd BG, which was struck by flak) being lost, and a further 170 bombers receiving varying degrees of damage.

The losses inflicted on VIII BC had not been eased by the arrival of the YB-40, proving that the multi-gunned B-17 concept was flawed. The additional weapons on each YB-40 did not add materially to the combined firepower that a group formation could bring to bear on attacking fighters, and a study of losses by VIII BC, had shown that it was the 'wounded' stragglers which were regularly attacked by the Luftwaffe. YB-40s were unable to protect these from concentrated attacks. YB-40 losses were not made good, and by the end of July 1943 they had all been either shot down or replaced by conventional B-17s.

Following the success of the Hüls raid, the 1st and 4th BWs were frustrated by a period of cloudy weather. On 26 June it finally improved sufficiently for 246 bombers to be sent against a large air depot in Villacoublay, in France. However, cloud returned to hamper the mission, only a dozen Fortresses actually dropped their bombs, and the 384th BG lost five B-17s near Paris.

On 4 July neither the weather nor the Independence Day celebrations stopped the Fortresses from making a triple attack on targets in France. Altogether, 192 B-17s from the 1st BW attacked the Gnôme and Rhône Aero engine factory at Le Mans and an aircraft factory at Nantes, while the 4th BW sent 45 bombers to hit the U-boat pens at La Pallice.

Shortly after noon the two 1st BW formations – flying parallel courses – crossed the French coast just east of the Cherbourg Peninsular, while the B-17s of the 4th BW headed along the Bay of Biscay coast for La Pallice. At 1230 hours the 1st BW formations passed over Laval, some 80 miles inland, then split into two groups. One headed for Le Mans and the other Nantes.

The latter force was subsequently intercepted by hordes of German fighters, which continued their attacks from the IP until the bombers were on their way home, some 35 miles north-west of the target. The 92nd BG's formation of 16 B-17s and three YB-40s bore the brunt of the head-on passes, and Lt John J Campbell's B-17 was lost. Six parachutes were seen to open, whilst a seventh seemed to only partially deploy.

The 92nd had welcomed back the 326th BS for this raid, the squadron having remained in the replacement combat crew training role longer than any other unit within the group. When the Luftwaffe intercepted

**B-17Gs of the 91st BG in formation.
Nearest aircraft is B-17G-50-BO
42-102509 *The LIBERTY RUN* from
the 401st BS, which failed to return
from Leipzig on 20 July 1944. Its
crew, led by Lt Arthur F Hultin, were
made PoWs
(*USAF via Tom Cushing*)**

the bombers, the 326th BS was subjected to repeated attacks. One of the
aircraft hit was B-17F 42-5910 *Ruthie*, named by pilot Lt Robert L
Campbell in honour of his wife. Coming off the target, the bomber lost
two fuel lines and its hydraulic system and flaps to cannon fire, whilst
another 20 mm shell wrecked the radio equipment after penetrating the
fuselage between the waist gun positions. Finally, ball turret gunner
Richard O Gettys was seriously wounded in the face, chest and groin by
yet another exploding cannon shell.

Despite his wounds, Gettys continued firing from the still serviceable
turret until he finally passed out – he was duly awarded the DSC for his
actions on this raid. Tail-gunner John C Ford was also slightly injured in
the leg during these attacks.

Campbell nursed *Ruthie* home to Alconbury, where he carried out a
textbook landing despite having had one tyre shot away. He kept the
badly damaged bomber on the runway for as long as he could, before
whirling the aircraft around in front of the control tower and coming to a
halt. *Ruthie* was scrapped on the spot, and Campbell and his crew issued
with replacement B-17F 42-29802, which they christened *Ruthie II*.

Whilst the Nantes raiders fought for their very survival, the Le Mans
force was also having to fend off the *Jagdwaffe*. Again encountering
intense fighter opposition just 15 minutes away from dropping their
bombs, these B-17 crews were lucky in that their target was further north-
east (and therefore closer to home), thus allowing them to pick up their
fighter escort a few minutes early, over Argentan.

For once the multiplicity of bomber attacks across France had seemed
to break up the concentrations of Luftwaffe fighters, and they were able to
account for just three per cent of the attacking force.

New groups continued to swell the ranks of VIII BC, and on 17 July a
record 332 bombers were sent to Hanover. With so many 'heavies' at Gen
Eaker's disposal, he now had the means to launch an all-out air offensive.
On the 23rd, Eighth Air Force mission planners were informed that clear
skies could be expected over Europe for several consecutive days, so VIII

BC was instructed to hastily prepare for the long-awaited series of attacks which would become known as 'Blitz Week', after the German word for 'lightning war'. The first raid would take place the very next day.

At briefings crews learned that for the first time they would be bombing targets in Norway. Groups from the 1st BW would target the incomplete aluminium, magnesium and nitrate plant of Nordisk Lettmetal at Heroya, south-east of Oslo. The mission was at the limits of the B-17's endurance, and in order to ensure that the bombers reached the target, there was no lengthy formation assembly. Instead, the lead B-17s simply set out on course immediately after take-off, cruising at reduced power at low altitude in order to allow the following aircraft to take their positions in the formation as they headed out over the North Sea.

Each wing flew with a gap of ten minutes, which in terms of distance gave them a separation of around 30 miles. This would allow time for the smoke from exploding bombs to clear the target area, thus giving the following strike forces a more precise aiming point for their bombardiers. Flak defences were believed to be poor this far north.

When the bombers reached their relatively low bombing altitude of 16,000 ft over the Skagerrak, they began flying above an overcast that lay below them at about 10,000 ft. The cloud blotted out the countryside, and was probably instrumental in keeping the Luftwaffe grounded at their bases in northern Denmark.

The bomb-bay doors swung open beneath the B-17s, but still there appeared no break in the cloud. Just as it began to look as if the crews would have to return to England with their bombs, Col William M Reid, CO of the 92nd BG, and the air commander for the mission, took the formation around for a second time and bombed through a sudden break in the cloud. This feat would earn him the Silver Star. The groups following had difficulty in picking out the MPI, so they were instructed to bomb the centre of the smoke pall, which by now was hanging almost stationary over the entire target area.

Altogether, 167 bombers bombed Heroya, completely devastating the industrial complex. The attack, which had taken place so far from England, caught the enemy by surprise, and many German dignitaries and Norwegian quislings who were attending a dedication ceremony at the plant were killed in the raid. No bombers were lost, although B-17F 42-3217 *Georgia Rebel* of the 535th BS/381st BG was so badly hit by flak that her crew were forced to land in neutral Sweden.

The next day one combat wing from the 1st BW was despatched to Kiel, whilst the remaining groups ventured to Hamburg to bomb the Blohm und Voss shipyards. Nearing the latter city, crews could see a towering 15,000-ft column of smoke – the result of fires still burning fol-

Lead navigator Lt Kermit B Cavedo of the 369th BS/306th BG liked the numerical connection between his squadron and the 'Fightin' 69th Regiment of World War 1, so using a little literary licence, he came up with the name 'Fightin'-Bitin', which he had applied to the nose of B-17F-50-BO 42-5426. *"FIGHTIN-BITIN"* was one four 306th BG B-17s lost on the raid on Kiel on 29 July 1943, when it carried 1Lt Donald R Winter's crew, but both the name and the emblem, showing two insects sparring, were adopted by the 369th BS. Its sister squadron, the 367th, which had the heaviest losses in VIII BC during October 1942-August 1943, was nicknamed the 'Clay Pigeons' *(Richards Collection)*

lowing a raid by RAF Bomber Command the previous night. Crews in the first elements managed to bomb before thick cloud added to the smoke, hitting the shipyards with great accuracy. However, Hamburg's notorious flak and fighter defences brought down 19 Fortresses, including seven from the unlucky 384th, whose squadrons filled the much-loathed low group position.

For the third day running Eaker despatched a large force against Germany, more than 300 'heavies' heading for Hanover and Hamburg on the 26th. However, thick cloud over East Anglia hampered formation assembly, and despite the recent innovation of 'splasher' beacons for forming up, many groups became scattered and had to be recalled. Only two combat wings pressed on to their targets, whilst other elements bombed targets of opportunity along the German coast.

Among the 92 Fortresses which successfully attacked Hanover were 17 B-17s and two YB-40s from the 92nd BG. Shortly before they crossed the coast, the formation came under frontal attack by Fw 190s. The first bomber lost was *Yo' Brother*, flown by Lt Alan E Hermance, which was seen to hit the water about ten minutes from the island of Nordenay with one engine on fire and the tail badly damaged. Capt Blair G Belongia's bomber then came under attack from seven Fw 190s, losing two of its engines. The pilot nursed the ailing B-17 back across the sea and successfully ditched about two miles off Sheringham, on the north Norfolk coast, where the crew were rescued by a passing fishing boat after an hour in the water.

Another 92nd BG B-17F in trouble was 42-29802 *Ruthie II*, piloted by 1Lt Robert L Campbell, who had brought the first *Ruthie* home from Nantes on 4 July fit only for scrap. Crew navigator Keith J Koske later recalled:

'We were on our way into the enemy coast when we were attacked by a group of Fw 190s. On their first pass I felt sure they had got us, for there was a terrific explosion overhead and the ship rocked badly. A second later, the top turret gunner, S/Sgt Tyre C Weaver, fell through the hatch and slumped to the floor at the rear of my nose compartment. When I got to him, I saw his left arm had been blown off at the shoulder and he was a mass of blood. I first tried to inject some morphine, but the needle was bent and I could not get it in.

'As things turned out, it was best I didn't give him any morphine. My first thought was to try and stop his loss of blood, so I tried to apply a tourniquet, but it was impossible as the arm was off too close to the shoulder. I knew he had to have the right kind of medical treatment as soon as possible, and we had almost four hours' flying time ahead of us, so there was no alternative. I opened the escape hatch, adjusted his 'chute for him and place the ripcord ring firmly in his right hand.

'He must have become excited and pulled the cord, opening the pilot 'chute in the updraught. I managed to gather it together and tuck it under his right arm, got him into a crouched position with legs through the hatch, made certain again that his good arm was holding the 'chute folds together, and toppled him out into space. I learned somewhat later from our ball gunner, James L Ford, that the 'chute opened OK. We were at 24,500 ft and 25 miles due west of Hanover, and our only hope was that he was found and given medical attention immediately.

'How was the flak at your altitude?' Lt McElwain and Capt 'Shorty' Miller, who were both 303rd BG navigators, compare heights at Molesworth on 18 July 1943 (*Harry D Gobrecht via Brian McGuire*)

'The bombardier, Asa J Irwin, had been busy with the nose guns, and when I got back up in the nose he was getting ready to toggle his bombs. The target area was one mass of smoke and we added our contribution. After we dropped our bombs, we were kept busy with the nose guns. However, all our attacks were from the tail, and we could do very little good. I had tried to use my interphone several times, but could get no answer. The last I remember hearing over it was shortly after the first attack, when someone was complaining about getting no oxygen. Except for what I thought to be some violent evasive action, we seemed to be flying OK.

'It was hours later, when we were 15 minutes from the enemy coast, that I decided to go up and check with the pilot and have a look around. I found Lt Campbell slumped down in his seat, a mass of blood, the back of his head blown off. This had happened two hours before, on the first attack. A shell had entered from the right side, crossed in front of John Morgan and hit Campbell in the head. Morgan was flying the plane with one hand, holding the half-dead pilot off with the other. Morgan told me he had to get Campbell out of his seat as the bomber could not be landed from the co-pilot's seat since the glass on that side was shattered so badly you could barely see out. We struggled for 30 minutes to get the fatally injured pilot down to the rear of the navigator's compartment, where the bombardier held him from slipping out of the open bomb hatch. Morgan was operating the controls with one hand and helping handle the pilot with the other.'

Despite his bomber having no workable hydraulics, radio or interphone, Morgan (a big 200-lbs, 6-ft, red-haired Texan, who had flown with the RCAF for seven months before transferring to the Eighth) had not only flown the B-17 to the target and out again, he had maintained formation throughout this time – an incredible feat for a pilot flying a badly damaged bomber one-handed. He landed *Ruthie II* safely at RAF Foulsham, in Norfolk, were Campbell died just 90 minutes later. The other crewmembers survived the ordeal, and weeks later word reached the 92nd BG that Tyre Weaver was also alive and well in a German hospital.

On 18 December 1943 listeners to the BBC's evening news heard that Flt Off (later 2Lt) John C Morgan (now with the 482nd BG) had received the Medal of Honor from Gen Ira Eaker in a special ceremony held at Eighth Air Force HQ. Morgan recounted the action of 26 July live on the radio.

'BLITZ WEEK' CONTINUES

Following a day's respite on 27 July, VIII BC resumed 'Blitz Week' on the morning of 28 July, when the 1st BW carried out an ambitious attack on aircraft factories at Kassel. However, the 182 'heavies' sent to the target were limited in their bombing because of cloud, which obscured the German city. On the way home they were attacked by fighters which fired rocket projectiles, eight inches in diameter, from tubes fitted under the fighter's wings. Fortunately for the bombers, the escorting P-47s saw off most of the fighters.

On 29 July, 91 B-17s of the 1st BW bombed the U-boat yards at Kiel and 81 'Forts' hit the Heinkel aircraft factory at Warnemunde. The next day VIII BC brought down the curtain on 'Blitz Week' when 186

Fortresses from the 1st and 4th BWs set out once again for the aircraft factories at Kassel – a round trip of some 600 miles. The weather was fine, and Thunderbolts fitted with long-range fuel tanks escorted the 'heavies' almost all the way to the target and back again. Without the presence of the 'Jugs' the losses suffered by the bombers would have been alarming, for the Fortress formations were hit by a ferocious onslaught from enemy fighters.

On the way to the target the B-17s had been aided by a strong wind which had given them 160 mph indicated airspeed. Now, on the homeward trip, the bombers had to buck this wind. Some were forced to ditch in the English Channel, whilst others had to make crash-landings all along the coast as one by one they ran low on fuel. Altogether, 12 Fortresses were lost, including some that were so badly damaged they never flew again. One such aircraft was *Patches* of the 384th BG, which crash-landed at the fighter airfield at Boxted (Station 150), in Essex. Salvageable parts from the bomber were subsequently used by other B-17s in the group.

On 31 July groups were stood down after a week of exhausting raids. VIII BC had lost around 100 aircraft and 90 combat crews, which had effectively reduced its combat strength to under 200 serviceable 'heavies'. Worse was still to come.

B-17F-30-BO 42-5077 *DELTA REBEL NO 2* of the 323rd BS/91st BG is 'awarded' the Air Medal. 41-24571 was the original *DELTA REBEL*, being delivered on 8 August 1942 and assigned to Lt George Birdsong's crew, but after diverting to Mitchel Field, New York, due to poor weather during a long training flight, transient maintenance taxied the *'REB* into two other aircraft, badly damaging all three! subsequently repaired, 41-24571 was renamed *INDIANAPOLIS WarBird* and issued to the 97th BG, and finally, the 49th BS/2nd BG, until 24 February 1943, when the entire squadron was wiped out at Steyr, in Austria. *DELTA REBEL NO 2* carried on into 1943 until Birdsong went home to Mississippi. This aircraft, and 2Lt Robert W Thompson's crew, failed to return from Gelsenkirchen on 12 August 1943 when 330 'heavies' hit targets in the Ruhr (*USAF*)

'BLACK THURSDAY' AND BEYOND

For almost two full weeks the badly battered bomb groups of VIII BC were stood down from operations in an attempt to make good the losses they had suffered during 'Blitz Week'. On 12 August they began their grim routine of striking targets on the continent once again when 330 bombers headed for the Ruhr. Weather was to dog the mission, and it caused many groups to seek targets of opportunity. Groups became strung out, which gave the *Jagdwaffe* the opportunity to strike at the widely dispersed formations. They hit the bombers time and again, with the 92nd and 384th BGs suffering particularly heavy losses – four and five aircraft respectively. In all, some 25 Fortresses were destroyed by flak or fighters, which was only one fewer than on 13 June, when VIII BC had suffered its greatest losses to date.

On 15 and 16 August the command participated in the 'Starkey' deception plan, which had been devised to make the enemy believe that an invasion of the French coast was imminent. It was hoped that such a ruse would relieve some of the pressure on Soviet forces on the eastern front, as well as halting the movement of German troops into Italy. The Fortress formations roamed across France, Belgium and Holland, dropping their deadly loads of bombs on long suffering German airfields. Friendly fighter support was generally described as 'excellent', and the Luftwaffe stayed largely on the ground.

The Field Order for Thursday, 17 August, called for an ambitious, and daring, strike on the aircraft factory at Regensburg and the ball-bearing plant at Schweinfurt. Brig Gen Robert Williams, commander of the 1st BW, would lead his force to the latter target, while Col Curtis E LeMay led the 4th BW to Regensburg. To minimise attacks from enemy fighters, LeMay's B-17s would fly on to North Africa after the target. The 1st BW, meanwhile, would fly a parallel course to Schweinfurt to further confuse the enemy defences, before returning to England after the raid.

Despite meticulous mission planning, Eaker knew the B-17 crews would have a running fight on their hands, but hoped that four P-47 groups detailed to escort the Regensburg raiders would help keep losses down. However, the 4th BW encountered the full force of the defending *Jagdwaffe* units due to thick inland mists delaying the departure of the 1st BW groups from their bases. The bombers eventually took off some three-and-a-half hours after the 4th BW had launched, the weather having effectively put paid to the planned two-pronged assault, which might have split the opposing fighter force.

The delay gave the Luftwaffe time to refuel and re-arm its fighters after dealing with the Regensburg force. Airborne again with time to spare, the *Jagdflieger* were quickly vectored onto the second wave of 'heavies' by their seasoned fighter controllers. They attacked the Schweinfurt force with the same ferocity that had seen them down 24 of the Regensburg raiders. This time, however, they went 12 better, shooting down no fewer than 36 Fortresses. The hardest hit units within the 1st BW on what became known as 'Black Thursday' to the surviving crews were the 381st and 91st BGs, which lost 11 and 10 B-17s respectively.

Despite being dealt such a crippling blow, VIII BC pressed on with its cycle of missions to France and the Low Countries, before returning to Germany once again on 6 September. A force of 338 B-17s was sent by Eaker to bomb the aircraft components factories at Stuttgart, although cloud interfered with formation assembly over England. Shortly after crossing the enemy coast the bombers came under sporadic attack, which was an ominous indication that the bulk of the fighter force was massing further inland for a concentrated strike.

Thick cloud also began to build up the nearing the formation got to the target, and the feeling among the B-17 crews was that the mission should be aborted. Brig Gen Robert B Travis, who had assumed command of the 1st BW from Brig Gen Williams, circled Stuttgart for approximately 30 minutes in a vain attempt to find the target. Many Fortresses failed to bomb, and 233 bombers released their ordnance on targets of opportunity whilst heading back westward towards to the enemy coast. By the time the B-17s were east of Paris, red lights had begun to show on the fuel gauges, and many crews began to wonder if they would ever make England. Fortunately, only three B-17s from the 92nd BG were forced to ditch in the sea, having exhausted their fuel supplies, while a fourth went down just two miles off the English coast.

REORGANISATION

On 13 September VIII BC's four bomb wings were formed into three bombardment divisions (BDs), each one organised into combat bombardment wings (CBWs). The nine groups in the 1st BW formed the 1st BD, commanded by Gen Williams. It now comprised the 1st CBW (91st, 351st, 381st and 398th BGs), 40th CBW (92nd, 305th and 306th BGs) and 41st CBW (303rd, 379th and 384th BGs). Later, the 92nd CBW was activated, operating for a short time until the 94th CBW was formed in December 1943. It comprised the 351st, 401st and 457th BGs.

In an effort to improve navigation and bombing within VIII BC, a single B-17F was equipped with a H_2S set as used with great success by RAF Bomber Command. Trialled under combat conditions for the first time by the 482nd BG on 23 September, the results proved to be so impressive that Eaker instructed that similarly equipped Fortresses should accompany the

Col Kermit D Stevens was CO of the 303rd BG between 19 July 1943 and 1 September 1944. He joined the Eighth Air Force at Savannah, Georgia, when first activated, and came to England with its nucleus in 1942. Stevens served as the Eighth's Operations Officer until he joined the 303rd BG. He led the group on a number of successful missions, and earned the Silver Star for Gallantry in action while leading the 1st BD in an attack on Le Bourget aerodrome on 16 August 1943 (*Harry D Gobrecht via Brian McGuire*)

B-17F-20-BO 41-24524 *The EAGLE'S WRATH* of the 323rd BS/91st BG and Lt Anthony G Arcaro's crew were lost on the 17 August 1943 raid on Schweinfurt. Some 27 B-17s from the 1st BW were so badly damaged on this day that they never flew again (*USAF*)

force of 305 bombers to Emden on 27 September. The latter target was ideal for radar bombing because of its proximity to water, which would show up reasonably well on the cathode ray tubes studied by the bombardier. In all, 244 bombers hit the target, but photo-reconnaissance later proved that only the H_2S-assisted formations had achieved a fair concentration of bombs on Emden. The other bomb patterns ranged as far away as five miles from the city itself.

A period of bad weather which followed gave technicians time to iron out some of the teething troubles before the bombers were despatched to Emden again on Monday, 2 October, with two H_2S-equipped aircraft from the 482nd BG. Brig Gen Robert W Travis led the mission in *Little America*, and this time the H_2S sets worked perfectly, although inexperience resulted in one Pathfinder Force (PFF) aircraft releasing its bombs too early, which saw many B-17s drop their loads short of the target. Winds also carried away smoke markers, disrupting the aim of the following formations.

Further radar bombing was delayed because the 482nd BG had insufficient aircraft (only eight B-17Fs were converted into H_2S carriers), and crews, to participate in yet another major mission, and with better weather conditions being found over western Germany, VIII BC reverted to visual attacks. On 4 October 361 bombers were despatched without PFF, and cloud over the target ruled out accurate bombing at any of the designated objectives. Twelve B-17s were shot down, and but for the strong P-47 escort, and a diversion mission flown by B-24s, losses would have been much higher.

Four days later the Fortresses went to Bremen, and in order to split the enemy fighter force, the 1st BD approached the target from Holland, while the 3rd BD crossed the North Sea and headed inland from the north-west. Meanwhile, the 2nd BD flew a long, curving, route over the North Sea to Vegesack. The *Jagdwaffe* waited for the P-47 escorts to withdraw, having exhausted their fuel, then hit the B-17s in strength. The 381st BG, flying in the dreaded low group position within the 1st BD formation, lost seven of its eighteen B-17s, including the lead ship.

1Lt Martin Andrews of the 423rd BS/306th BG landed B-17F-25-VE 42-5841 *EST NULLA VIA IN VIA VIRTUTI* (Latin for 'There is no way impossible to courage') at Magadino airfield, near Ticino, in southern Switzerland, on 6 September 1943 after running low on fuel on the Stuttgart mission. Bereft of Swiss navigation charts, 2Lt C Gordon Bowers, navigator, relied on his silk 'escape' map to give Andrews an accurate heading to the neutral country. 42-5841 was later flown to the Emmen test and experimental centre, and at the end of the war Swiss groundcrews performed an engine change before the aircraft was handed back to the AAF (*Hans-Heiri Stapfer*)

On 9 October 378 'heavies' were sortied on the day's various raids, which saw three targets bombed. A total of 115 aircraft from the 1st and 41st CBWs were despatched to the Arado aircraft component plant at Anklam, near Peenemünde. These bombers acted as a diversion force for 263 'heavies' sent to attack the port of Gydnia, on the Polish border, and the Focke-Wulf plant at Marienburg. The Anklam force lost 14 B-17s in total, all of which came from the 1st CBW.

Intelligence sources now confirmed that the Luftwaffe's fighter strength was on the increase, despite the implementation of the *Pointblank* directive in June. In fact, at the beginning of October the Luftwaffe had 1646 single- and twin-engined fighters available for the defence of the Reich – some 400 more than before the *Pointblank* campaign had commenced! Reacting to this disappointing news, VIII BC took the decision to attack the crucial ball-bearing plant at Schweinfurt for the second time in three months.

As one of the best defended sites in Germany, and well out of range of VIII FC's fighter escorts, Schweinfurt was undoubtedly the most feared target destination amongst bomber crews at that point in the war. VIII BC had only visited the city once before, on 17 August, and 360 airmen had not returned. However, Eighth Air Force mission planners knew that they had to stem the flow of fighters reaching the *Jagdwaffe*, and it was hoped that if the bombers could deliver a single decisive blow to the Schweinfurt plant, production by the enemy's aircraft industry would be suitably affected.

B-17F-15-VE 42-5763 *BOMB-BOOGIE* of the 401st BS/91st BG. On 6 September 1943 this Fortress, flown by 1Lt Elwood D Arp's crew, was one of 45 'heavies' shot down on the mission to the aircraft components factories at Stuttgart (*USAF*)

Two B-17Gs and B-17F-BO-50-VE 42-6174 *Home-Sick Angel/Stripped for Action* (right) of the 422nd BS/305th BG prepare to take off from Cheveston. On 23 May 1945 42-6174, now named *Swing Shift*, transferred to the Night Leaflet Squadron (*USAF*)

306th BG B-17s weave their way through heavy flak over Schweinfurt on 14 October 1943. This group lost ten Fortresses during the mission, which was the second highest loss tally within the 1st BD – the 305th BG was the worst hit, having 16 Fortresses destroyed (*Richards*)

B-17F-115-BO 42-30727 *"FIGHTIN-BITIN"* of the 367th 'Clay Pigeons' BS/306th BG, and Lt William C Bisson's crew, failed to return from Schweinfurt on 14 October 1943 when flak knocked out two of its engines and fighters riddled the rear fuselage. S/Sgt Thompson E Wilson, tail gunner, and four others, were killed in action, whilst 2Lt Charles R Stafford, co-pilot, who exited through the side cockpit window, and four crewmen in the aft section were made PoW (*Richards*)

On 13 October Brig Gen Orvil Anderson of VIII BC instructed his staff to send out warning orders to all three bomb division HQs, giving details of a large mission to Schweinfurt for the following day. Anderson hoped to launch 420 Fortresses and Liberators in a three-pronged attack on the city. The 1st and 3rd BDs were to cross Holland some 30 miles apart, while the third task force, composed of 60 B-24s, would fly to the south on a parallel course. The 923-mile trip would last just over seven hours, so B-17s of the 1st BD which were not equipped with 'Tokyo tanks' (extra fuel cells in the wings) would have to carry an additional fuel tank in the bomb-bay. This effectively reduced the aircraft's already modest bombload.

Each division would be escorted by a P-47 group, while a third group would provide withdrawal support from 60 miles inland to halfway across the Channel. Finally, two squadrons of RAF Spitfire Mk IXs were to provide cover for the stragglers five minutes after the main force had left the withdrawal area, and other RAF squadrons would be on standby for action if required. Despite these precautions, 370 miles of the route would be flown without fighter support. The 92nd BG, which would be flying in the van of the 40th CBW, would lead the 1st BD.

The unpredictable autumn weather intervened before the bombers had even taken off, hampering the B-24s' assembly, and then finally ruling out their participation altogether. The remaining bombers finally took off after a 25th BG Mosquito, cruising over the continent at 35,000 ft, radioed back to VIII BC that all of central Germany was clear of cloud.

The 40th CBW led the 1st BD over the coast of England, and en route to the target the division had 15 of its 164 B-17s abort due to mechanical problems or through formation separation in cloud. Assembly diminished the Fortresses' vital fuel reserves (especially of those aircraft forced to carrying bombs externally in order to make up for the lack of internal space due to the fitment of bomb-bay fuel tanks), and many were forced to dump their wing-mounted bombs in the Channel, or abort the mission altogether.

By the time the division finally entered the target area, the 1st BD had already lost 36 bombers to enemy action, and a further 20 had turned back. Most of the groups had been torn to shreds, and some of the formations were skeletal at best. The

306th had lost ten of its 21 Fortresses, and by the time the 305th BG could finally see the city of Schweinfurt, 12 miles in the distance, it had lost the entire low squadron of five aircraft, as well as the majority of its high and lead squadrons. Only three of the original 18 aircraft from the group remained, and despite being joined by a lone Fortress from another group, it was still not enough for effective bombing to take place.

Realising that his now emaciated force was of little use in its present form, 305th BG formation leader Maj G G Y Normand decided to join the depleted 92nd and 306th BG formations for the bomb run.

Of the 37 Fortresses in the 40th CBW that had crossed the Channel, only 16 remained – and worse was to follow. At 1439 the 91st BG began dropping its bombs on the streets, houses and factories of Schweinfurt. The 91st was to claim the best overall bombing results for the 1st BD on this day, although the 351st BG from the same wing (1st CBW) was deemed to have been the most accurate. Indeed, Capt H D Wallace, squadron bombardier in part of the group's formation, placed all of his bombs within 1000 ft of the MPI.

The three surviving bombers in the 305th BG, meanwhile, mistakenly bombed the centre of the city. Immediately after 'bombs away', the group's 13th victim was claimed by fighters, leaving only Maj Normand and another B-17 from the 18 that had originally set out from Chelveston. The two survivors turned away from the target and followed the lead group home.

The 40th CBW dropped its bombs and headed in the direction of the 1st CBW, which was now making for the French border. The third and final wing, the 41st, added its bombs to the conflagration, before turning off the target to allow the 3rd BD, flying six minutes behind, to take its turn – the city of Schweinfurt soaked up over 483 short tons of high explosives and incendiaries. After dropping their bombs, the B-17s performed a 180-degree turn around Schweinfurt, before heading west. Whilst still in the process of changing course, the 1st BD was hit heavily by a full *gruppe* of Fw 190s, who quickly singled out the trailing 41st CBW. The leading 379th BG lost four B-17s during the fighters' first pass.

Reeling from the series of devastating attacks inflicted upon its formations, the surviving 1st BD bomber crews headed for the rally point and began reforming into combat wings for the return flight over Germany and France. Amongst the bombers to make it back to the French coast were the two surviving aircraft from the 305th BG. Luckily for them, they had met with little fighter opposition on the way home, which was just as well for they had used up almost all their ammunition before they had even reached target.

Gen Maurice 'Mo' Preston (right), CO of the 379th BG, listens to Maj 'Rip' Rohr upon his return as leader of the group during the disastrous mission to Schweinfurt on 14 October 1943 (*USAF*)

B-17F-75-DL 42-3540 *Bacta-th' Sac* of the 535th BS, was the first G-model assigned to the 381st BG, on 16 September 1943. 42-3540 and 2Lt Warren C Hess's crew failed to return from Leverkusen, in the Ruhr, on 1 December 1943. One of four bombers lost on this date, two of the crew subsequently evaded, one was killed in action and seven were made PoW (*USAF*)

B-17F-15-VE 42-97504 *Mary Lou* was assigned to the 323rd BS/91st BG on 23 January 1944. On its 70th mission, on 14 October 1944, it suffered battle damage at Freiberg and crash-landed at Bassingbourn upon its return (*via Robert M Foose*)

The Fortresses' return to England was hampered by the same 'soupy' weather that had dogged their departure, and at 1640 hours the 1st BD at last crossed the Channel coast, followed just five minutes later by the 3rd BD.

Altogether, the 1st BD had lost a record 45 Fortresses on the raid, with the 305th BG losing 16 and the 306th BG 10. The 92nd BG had seen six of its B-17s shot down, with a seventh written off in a crash-landing at Aldermaston. The 379th and 384th BGs had also lost six Fortresses apiece in combat, with a further three crews from the latter group abandoning their aircraft over England. The 303rd BG lost two B-17s, including one which crash-landed after the crew had baled out near Riseley, whilst the 91st, 351st and 381st BGs each lost one Fortress apiece. The 3rd BD had lost 15 aircraft.

The latest Schweinfurt raid had cost VIII BC 60 Fortresses and 600 men. Five B-17s had crashed in England as a result of their battle-damaged condition, whilst 12 more were destroyed in forced landings, or had been so badly damaged that they had to be written off. Of the returning

bombers 121 required repairs, and another five fatal casualties and 43 wounded crewmen were removed from the aircraft once on the ground.

The results of the raid were generally disappointing, and in no way offset the loss of so many men and machines. Only 88 of the 1222 bombs dropped actually fell on the plants, causing production at the Kugelfischer plant – largest of the five sites attacked – to be interrupted for just six weeks. Indeed, although Schweinfurt was bombed on numerous occasions after this raid, the German war machine never lacked for ball-bearings throughout the remainder of the

B-17F-27-BO 41-24605 *KNOCK-OUT DROPPER* of the 359th BS/303rd BG was the first Eighth Air Force B-17 to complete both 50 (on 16 November 1943) and 75 combat missions (27 March 1944). *KNOCK-OUT DROPPER* was scrapped at Stillwater, Oklahoma, in July 1945 (*Lt Col Harry D Gobrecht*)

conflict. As with many other industries within the increasingly beleaguered Third Reich, the dispersal of ball-bearing factories ensured a ready supply of these crucially important components, whilst a combination of careful husbanding of resources and outstanding technical innovation by industrial designers meant that certain forms of machinery needed less or no ball-bearings at all.

The day after the second Schweinfurt mission all heavy bomb groups were stood down in order to lick their wounds, the B-17s having their various flak and bullet holes patched up. Replacement crews were also sent in, but the grave losses, combined with a spell of bad weather, restricted the Eighth Air Force to just two more missions in October. Then, on 3 November, VIII BC was assigned Wilhelmshaven. Altogether, 555 bombers, led by a handful of H_2X radar-equipped B-17Gs from the 482nd BG, were despatched to attack the German port. H_2X (which was given the cover name *Mickey Mouse*, later shortened to just *Mickey*, by the AAF) was a recently-developed American version of the British H_2S bombing aid. Due to scarcity of equipment, just 12 aircraft were fitted with the nose-mounted radar scanner.

A P-38 escort kept losses to a minimum and earned the praise of the bomber crews, who were glad to see their 'little friends' for the entire duration of the flight.

B-17F-10-VE 42-5729 *Buccaneer* of the 401st BS/91st BG is seen taking off from Bassingbourn. This B-17F first served as *The Piccadilly Commando* in the 369th BS/306th BG between 18 February and 7 September 1943. *Buccaneer* was returned to the USA in March 1944 (*USAF*)

B-17G-15-DL 42-37805 was assigned to the 525th BS/379th BG at Kimbolton on 2 December 1943, where it was coded 'FR-R' and named *Carol Dawn* – it was later transferred to the 527th BS and re-coded 'FO-B'. *Carol Dawn* survived the war, having twice had to put down on the continent when returning from missions, and the veteran bomber ended its days at Kingman, Arizona, in December 1945 (*Charles L Brown*)

On 5 November the Eighth was again out in force when 374 Fortresses were despatched to the iron foundry works and marshalling yards at Gelsenkirchen, led by five *Oboe* Mk I radar-equipped pathfinders. For two weeks afterwards the weather grew worse, and resulted in many abortive missions. It was not until 11 November that VIII BC bombed a German target again when Münster was attacked for the first time since a disastrous raid on 10 October by the 3rd BW.

For much of early November the airfields in England had been socked in by fog, rain and high winds, but on the morning of the 16th the bad weather at last lifted and a mission to Norway went ahead as scheduled. Since their introduction the previous month, the handful of H_2X and *Oboe* sets had been proving troublesome, and the break in the weather gave crews the opportunity to bomb visually.

The 1st BD attacked the molybdenum mines at Knaben, while the 3rd BD targeted a generating plant in the Rjukan Valley. The raids caused great damage, and resulted in a complete stoppage of the entire manufacturing process of molybdenum – intelligence sources had indicated that both targets were connected with German heavy water experiments, which in turn were aimed at giving the Nazis the ability to create nuclear weapons.

One of the bombers involved in this mission was B-17F 41-24605 *KNOCKOUT DROPPER* of the 359th BS/ 303rd BG. Flown by Lt John P Manning on this occasion, the aircraft's safe return to Molesworth made it the first Fortress to complete 50 missions in the ETO.

On 18 November 127 'heavies' were despatched to Gelsenkirchen once again, although continued unreliability with the *Oboe* sets aboard the leading Fortresses saw the formation directed too far north of the target. After an unsuccessful battle with the elements, the B-17s were forced to return to England. The bad weather continued over the next few days, although it did not prevent RAF Bomber Command bombing Berlin on the night of 22 November. This mission led to the scheduling of an American follow-up raid on the German capital the very next day, but the weather deteriorated once again and the raid was cancelled just before take-off. On 26 November, 633 bombers – the largest formation ever assembled by the Eighth – were directed against targets as far apart as Bremen and Paris. Two new B-17 groups, the 401st and 447th, had joined the 1st BD earlier in November, and the 401st made its combat debut on this maximum effort day.

Led by Col Harold W Bowman, the 401st BG helped swell the 1st BD's force to 505 B-17s, whose crews were briefed to bomb the port area of Bremen, while the 3rd BD headed for Paris. The Fortresses sent to hit the German city endured persistent attacks by up to 100 *Jagdwaffe* fighters of every description, including Stuka dive-bombers! Flak was heavy over Bremen itself, and the target was covered with cloud, so bombing results could not be determined. Some 86 enemy fighters were claimed destroyed, 26 of them by B-17 gunners. However, 29 Fortresses and five fighters were lost in return.

Bremen was scheduled to be hit again on the 29th, but poor weather over Germany saw the bombers recalled. Twenty-four later, Col Budd J Peaslee led a partially successful PFF attack on Solingen, after which ground haze over eastern England effectively grounded the VIII BC until 11 December. With a break in the weather on this day, a mixed force of B-17s and B-24s followed radar-equipped aircraft to Emden, where they bombed the docks and the industrial area for the loss of 17 'heavies'.

Two days later the Fortresses returned to Bremen for the first of three raids that month on the beleaguered German port. Of the 710 aircraft despatched, 649 bombed the port areas of Bremen and Hamburg, as well as the U-boat yards at Kiel. This was the first VIII BC mission in which more than 600 'heavies' had actually made it to the targets.

B-17G-1-BO 42-31033 *PEE TAY KUN* of the 613th BS/401st BS, which crash-landed at Deenthorpe on 16 December 1943. This aircraft, and 1Lt Stephen J Nasen's crew, failed to return from Oschersleben, in Germany, on 11 January 1944. Two crew were killed in action and eight made PoW (*via Mike Bailey*)

The Eighth Air Force was stood down on 23 December, but missions resumed on Christmas Eve when B-17s were sent to destroy mysterious targets in France which went under the code-name *Noball*. Crews speculated what the concrete sites were, and many believed them to be 'rocket' installations for Hitler's new 'secret weapons'. British Intelligence soon revealed them to be launch sites for 'V Weapons' – pilotless rockets, packed with a high-explosive warhead in the nose, that were fired across the Channel in the general direction of London. Allied sources in Occupied Europe had revealed that 70 such sites were under construction along the French coast, and all-out raids against these installations were ordered at once. On 24 December 670 'heavies' attacked 23 V1 sites in the Pas de Calais, returning without loss.

On Christmas Day no Eighth Air Force missions were flown, and festivities got into full swing. However, the war was never very far away, and preparations were already being made for the next strike as soon as the weather improved. On 30 December 658 'heavies' attacked the oil plant at Ludwigshafen. Altogether, 23 bombers were lost on the mission. On New Year's Eve almost 500 bombers made all-out attacks on airfields in France, the day's operations seeing 25 'heavies' fall to the deadly combination of flak and fighters. No fewer than nine of the downed B-17s came from the 351st BG, and one of those lost was the group lead aircraft, flown by Maj John R Blaylock, CO of the 510th BS. His crew also included Group CO, Col William A Hatcher Jr, who was later reported to be a PoW.

Frustratingly for crews, 1944 started much as 1943 had finished, with fog and rain grounding the bombers until 4 January, when over 500 'heavies' headed for the continent. The 1st BD went to Kiel, while unescorted groups in the 3rd BD spearheaded an assault on enemy airfields in France. Included in the force on this day was the 91st BG, whose

A formation of 306th BG B-17Gs is seen in early 1944. Closest to the camera is B-17G-20-BO 42-31454 *St Anthony,* which joined the 368th BS at Thurleigh on 30 December 1943. It survived its tour of missions and was scrapped on 31 January 1946 (*USAF*)

participation in the mission made it the first bomb group in the Eighth to reach 100 missions. This accolade had come at a heavy price, however, for the 'Ragged Irregulars' of Bassingbourn had lost more aircraft and crews on missions than any other group. The next day 426 'heavies' again struck at targets in France and Germany.

COMMAND CHANGES

The 5 January missions proved to be the last under the auspices of VIII BC. With the establishment of the Fifteenth Air Force in Italy, whose role in the MTO would be very similar to the Eighth's in the ETO, the AAF decided to embrace both air forces in a new central HQ called US Strategic Air Forces in Europe (USSTAF), at Bushey Hall in Teddington, Middlesex – previously HQ, Eighth Air Force. Former Eighth Air Force chief, Maj Gen Carl 'Tooey' Spaatz, returned to England from the MTO to take command of the new organisation, bringing with him ex-4th BW Commander, Lt Gen James H Doolittle. Famous for his surprise raid on Tokyo in April 1942 (for which he won a Medal of Honor), Doolittle assumed command of the Eighth Air Force from Lt Gen Ira C Eaker, who in turn transferred to the MTO.

On 7 January 420 B-17s bombed the I G Farben Industrie plant at Ludwigshafen, the raid costing the Eighth 12 bombers and seven fighters. Considerable damage was caused to various chemical and substitute war material plants at this site, however. The twin city of Mannheim was also heavily hit, with damage being caused to the engineering and transport industries.

Four days later a maximum effort comprising all three bomb divisions was planned for the aircraft factories at Waggum, Halberstadt and Oschersleben, all of which were situated in the Brunswick area – a city notorious for its flak and fighter defences. All bombing was to be carried out using visual sightings, although the unpredictable nature of the weather at that time of the year meant that crews were also briefed to bomb the city using PFF techniques if necessary. Bad weather dogged the mission from the start, causing most of the fighter escort to abort prior to their rendezvous with the bombers. In turn, the 2nd and 3rd BDs were ordered to turn back because of the paucity of escorts, although the 1st BD was left to continue due to its close proximity to Brunswick.

The latter division was being led on this raid by the 303rd BG, whilst Brig Gen Robert Travis flew as Task Force Commander aboard 359th BS B-17F 41-24635 *The Eight Ball*, piloted by the squadron CO, Lt Col Bill Calhoun. Less than 50 miles from Brunswick, the formation was bounced by over 200 fighters just as its passed the Dummer Lake. They continued their ferocious attacks from all angles until just before the B-17s commenced their bombing run. Once the 'heavies' had

During March and April 1943, crew battle armour developed by Col Malcolm C Grow (Chief Surgeon of the Eighth Air Force) proved a worthy innovation. Gunners Bill Dickson, right, and Ed Lawler, left (who is wearing one of the new armoured flak vests), pose in front of B-17F-75-BO 42-29921 *OKLAHOMA OKIE*. This aircraft joined the 324th BS/91st BG at Bassingbourn on 23 May 1943, and it was lost, along with 2Lt Baynard T G Dudley's crew, on a raid to Cognac, in France, on 31 December 1943. Five crew were killed in action, four were made PoW and one waist gunner evaded (*USAF*)

A Messerschmitt Bf 110 attacks a formation of 91st BG B-17s approaching their target on 22 January 1944 (*USAF via Robert M Foose*)

B-17G-1-BO 42-31047 *WOLVERINE* of the 535th BS/381st BG. An early G-model, it has neither cheek guns nor Plexiglas waist window panels. On its 19th mission, on 30 January 1944, *WOLVERINE* and 2Lt Robert P Deering's crew failed to return from Brunswick. Eight men were killed in action and two were made PoW (*USAF via Mike Bailey*)

dropped their ordnance and pulled off the target, the fighters attacked again. To some crews it looked as if 'planes kept falling, spinning and exploding'. The 303rd lost ten B-17s and the 351st seven.

Eight months later, in August, all the 1st BD groups which took part in the Brunswick raid on this day were awarded Presidential Unit Citations.

On 21 January the 457th BG, nicknamed the 'Fireball Outfit', and commanded by Col James R Luper, arrived at Glatton (Station 130), in Huntingdonshire. The group became a part of the 94th CBW, which also included the 351st at Polebrook and the 401st at Deenthorpe (Station 128), in Northamptonshire.

Vast banks of strato-cumulus clouds which covered most of Germany prevented visual bombing for the next few weeks, so the B-17 groups reverted to attacking targets in France. One exception to this routine occurred on 30 January when the Eighth Air Force returned to the aircraft factories at Brunswick. A record 778 'heavies' were despatched, and bombing was carried out using PFF techniques.

Of the 29 missions flown during January and February 1944, 13 were to V1 rocket sites. These strikes were no longer regarded as 'milk runs' by the groups, for the Germans had moved in additional flak batteries once the installations' vulnerability to air attack was exposed. The AAF's response was to raise the bombing altitude to 20,000 ft.

'BIG WEEK' AND 'BIG B'

Since arriving in the ETO, Gen Doolittle had been biding his time, waiting for a period of relatively fine weather in which to mount a series of raids on the German aircraft industry. Finally, AAF meteorologists informed him that the week 20-25 February 1944 would be ideal for such an offensive, which was duly dubbed 'Big Week' within the Eighth. On the 20th, a force of over 800 'heavies' was assembled, and the 1st and 2nd BDs were briefed to hit the Bf 109 plant at Leipzig, which had been bombed only a few hours earlier by the RAF. The 3rd BD, meanwhile, would visit Posen, in Poland.

As the 1st BD formation crossed into Germany, it was opposed by single- and twin-engined Luftwaffe aircraft of almost every type, including Ju 87s, He 111s, Do 17s and Fw 189s. The German pilots adopted single-

'Loading the airmail addressed to Hitler'. Groundcrew prepare to load 500-lb bombs aboard B-17F-75-BO 42-29931 *SATAN'S WORKSHOP* of the 360th BS/303rd BG for a raid on Germany. This aircraft, and Lt George E Underwood's crew, failed to return from Bernburg on 22 February 1944 when the B-17 ditched in the Channel. All ten crew perished (*Lt Col Harry D Gobrecht via Brian Maguire*)

75

engined fighter tactics in an effort to gain favourable attacking positions, and they flew right through the formations and slow rolled while shooting. In a last ditch effort to deter the 1st BD, the defenders also tried cable-bombing methods, but with little success.

Leading the 1st BD was the 401st BG, with its CO, Col Harold W Bowman, at the head of the 94th CBW. He led his formation on to the briefed point west of Brunswick, before diverging to bomb the target. Despite a heavy flak barrage during the bomb run, which badly damaged Bowman's aircraft, the formation succeeded in dropping its bombs directly onto the MPI, as the colonel recalls;

'Because the weather was uncertain we were provided with a PFF crew especially trained for instrument bombing. The weather en route was indeed bad, and preparations were made for aiming by instrument means, but as we approached the target area the clouds opened up to "scattered", and a visual sighting was made. The result was, for our group, 100 per cent of our bombs within 1000 ft of the aiming point.'

Direct hits were achieved on the principal assembly shop at the Erla Maschinenwerk Messerschmitt production factory, whilst its other large assembly building on the same site was also observed to be on fire as the bombers left the target area.

Such success came at a price, however, and no fewer than three Medals of Honor were awarded to 1st BD crewmembers. This was the only occasion in Eighth Air Force history when multiple medals were awarded for a single day's action involving men flying from Britain. Only one survived to collect his medal, 1Lt William R Lawley Jr of the 364th BS/305th BG being decorated for nursing his crippled B-17G (42-38109) back to England after he had suffered serious facial injuries at the target when the cockpit was struck by a cannon round. The impact of the shell killed his

Lt Thomas H Gunn of the 323rd BS/91st BG brought B-17G-20-DL 42-37938 *Betty Lou's Buggy* safely back to Bassingbourn on 19 April 1944 after sustaining heavy damage from Bf 109s over the Focke-Wulf assembly plant at Eschwege, near Kassel. Fighters holed the left wing fuel tank, put a turbo out, damaged an engine, knocked out the elevators and left aileron and exploded shells in the nose, cockpit, bombbay and fin. Gunn could only control direction by using the engines, and had to apply full right aileron to keep the B-17 level. Only the co-pilot and navigator were wounded. Here, Robert D Smith, Gunn's tail gunner, inspects the damage to the fin of *Betty Lou's Buggy*, caused by a cannon shell which severed the rudder controls. The Fortress was repaired, re-assigned to the 324th BS and survived the war, only to be cut up for scrap at Kingman, Arizona, in December 1945 (*USAF*)

B-17F-20-DL 42-3040 *MISS OUACHITA* of the 323rd BS/91st BG, and 2Lt Spencer K Osterberg's crew, failed to return from a raid (its 18th mission) on Gutersloh, in Germany on 22 February 1944. This B-17, which had previously served with both the 303rd BG and the 369th BS/306th BG, was shot down by Maj Heinz 'Pritzl' Bär, *Kommandeur* of II./JG 1, who was flying a Fw 190. He is seen here looking over the wreckage at Bexten, near Saltzbergen, where the B-17 crashlanded. Note that he is wearing a captured American A-2 leather jacket, whilst the pilot stood behind him also sports an ex-AAF fur-lined jacket. Two crewmen were killed in this action, and the remaining eight made PoW. *MISS OUACHITA* was deemed repairable by a German salvage team, but she was strafed and destroyed by US fighters before the it could be retrieved. The top scoring NCO pilot of the Battle of Britain, Bär claimed his 200th victory just two months after downing *MISS OUACHITA*, on 22 April 1944. He ended the war as the top scoring jet ace of World War 2 with 16 kills, and was eighth overall in the list of *experten*, with 220 confirmed victories. Bär was killed in a light aircraft crash in 1957 (*USAF*)

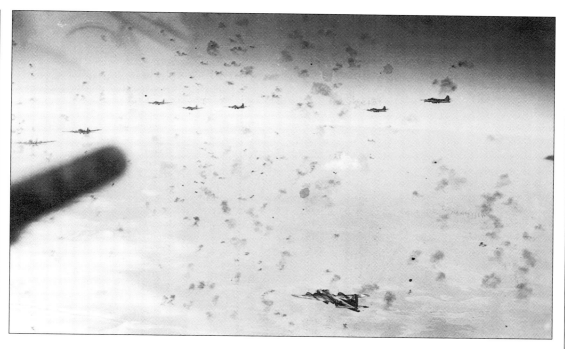

B-17s of the 457th BG fly through heavy flak over Schweinfurt on 24 February 1944 (*USAF*)

B-17G-20-VE 42-97622 *PAPER DOLLIE* of the 358th BS/303rd BG is seen following a crash at Molesworth on 1 March 1944. Repaired, it was finally written off on 23 July at Bishops Waltham, in Hampshire – two of Flt Off C M Miller's crew were killed and the other seven returned to duty. The aircraft was salvaged two days later (*USAF via Robert M Foose*)

co-pilot and injured a further seven crewmen. Lawley somehow nursed the now single-engined bomber back to England, despite lapsing in and out of consciousness.

The two posthumous awards of the Medal of Honor went to airmen who endured a similar experience. Navigator 2Lt Walter E Truemper and ball turret gunner Sgt Archie Mathies (from the 510th BS/351st BG) managed to keep B-17G 42-31763 *Ten Horsepower* in the air after a well-aimed burst by an attacking fighter struck the cockpit. The co-pilot was killed and the pilot grievously wounded to the point where he could not fly the badly damaged bomber. Rather than bale out and leave the pilot to die in the resulting crash, the two men chose to try and fly the B-17 back to their Polebrook base.

Once in the vicinity of the Northamptonshire air station, Truemper and Mathies instructed the crew to take to their parachutes, whilst they attempted to land the bomber. After two abortive attempts, the third one saw the Fortress stall and plough into a field near the base. The pilot was still alive when rescuers extricated him from the wreckage, although he died soon afterwards. Mathies and Truemper had been killed outright in the crash.

Despite the significant losses of the 20th, 'Big Week' had only just begun, and the following day the 'heavies' were again sent out in force. The bomber stream was swelled by 36 B-17s of the 457th BG, who were sent to attack the aircraft factories at Brunswick on their debut mission. However, thick cloud obscured the mission's primary objective, and bombing had to be completed using PFF techniques. Many groups chose instead to attack targets of opportunity, and airfields and aircraft depots were heavily bombed.

The following day the elements were responsible for collisions during assembly, and the 3rd BD was forced to abandon the mission completely. However, the 1st BD, led by the CO of the 379th BG, Col 'Mo' Preston, continued to the Junkers' works at Oschersleben. Enemy fighter interceptions were high, despite the hope that a simultaneous attack on Regensburg by the Fifteenth Air Force would split the German fighter force. The 1st BD lost 39 Fortresses during the day's raids, including seven from the 306th BG.

On 23 February bad weather kept the bombers on the ground. It allowed maintenance crews to work tirelessly around the clock to get every possible B-17 ready for the huge 800-aircraft mission planned by Doolittle for the following day. As part of this maximum effort, the 1st BD sent 231 B-17s to bomb the dreaded ball-bearing factories at Schweinfurt, although on this occasion 'only' 11 Fortresses were lost.

The 25th marked the culmination of 'Big Week', with the Eighth Air Force flying its deepest raid into Germany thus far. The 1st BD was assigned the Messerschmitt experimental and assembly plants at Augs-

A scattered trail of propaganda leaflets leads to B-17G-15-VE 42-97469 *BUSY-BABY* of the 527th BS/379th BG, parked at dispersal at Kimbolton on 8 April 1944. This aircraft, which lived up to its name by enjoying a long and a varied career in the Eighth Air Force, finished up at RAF Binbrook in December 1944, where it was declared war weary on 11 January 1945. The bomber was eventually scrapped at Kingman, Arizona, in December 1945 (*USAF via Mike Bailey*)

burg and the fighter plant at Stuttgart. Some 680 'heavies' were sortied, with the mission being flown in conjunction with a Fifteenth Air Force attack on Regensburg. All three divisions of the Eighth exacted a heavy toll on the German aircraft plants for the loss of 31 bombers.

Thereafter, cloud banks over the continent brought a premature end to 'Big Week', which gave higher command time to assess the results, and implications, of their actions over the past five days.

Although the Eighth had flown some 3300 bomber sorties and dropped 6000 tons of bombs during 'Big Week', post-mission reconnaissance photos of the various targets hit revealed that the destruction wreaked by the AAF had not been as great as had at first been thought. However, Doolittle and his staff officers still believed that the Eighth had dealt the German aircraft industry a severe blow, and they now felt confident to strike at Berlin, or 'Big B' as it was known to Eighth Air Force crews.

The raid on the German capital was originally scheduled for 3 March, but this had to be aborted due to bad weather. The following day crews went back to their briefing rooms to find that 'Big-B' was on again, although cloud cover resulted in yet another general recall. Despite this, three squadrons from the 3rd BD pressed on to the capital alone, and subsequently dropped the first American bombs to fall on Berlin.

On 6 March the Eighth despatched 730 'heavies', escorted by almost 800 fighters, to Berlin. The 1st BD was assigned the VKF ball-bearing plant at Erkner, in the eastern suburbs of the city, and they were intercepted over the Dummer Lake by the *Jagdwaffe*. The leading groups – the 91st, 92nd and 381st BGs – bore the brunt of the attacks, although the 457th BG also endured a series of head-on passes that saw one Bf 109 crash headlong into 2Lt Roy E Graves' B-17. The combined wreckage then struck 2Lt Eugene H Whalen's Fortress, before all three aircraft plummeted to earth.

Although B-17 gunners and AAF fighter pilots claimed over 170 German fighters destroyed between them, the 'heavies' had suffered record losses – 69 bombers destroyed, including 18 from the 1st BD, and a further 102 seriously damaged.

Just 72 hours later 600 bombers flew the third raid on 'Big B' that week, the 3rd BD returning to the VKF ball-bearing plant at Erkner as a follow-up to the mission on the

B-17G-1-VE 42-39785 *THRU hel'en hiwater* was assigned to the 358th BS/303rd BG on 18 October 1943. It was lost, along with 2Lt Roy A Larson's crew, during the mission to Hamm on 22 April 1944. Four men were killed in action and six were made PoW. A year earlier, this B-17 had buzzed Yankee Stadium in New York during the World Series, much to the exasperation of Mayor La Guardia (*USAF*)

6th. The 1st BD was also involved, flying in the middle of the formation, with Liberators bringing up the rear. The 3rd BD encountered the fiercest fighter opposition on the raid, which cost 37 Fortresses. On 9 March the Eighth was again despatched to Berlin, some 300 B-17s reaching Berlin only to find that 10/10ths cloud over the target prevented any visual bombing from taking place. The Luftwaffe was notable for its absence throughout the duration of this raid.

On 22 March 1944 almost 800 B-17s and B-24s returned to Berlin, led by H$_2$X-equipped bombers flying their last mission under the control of the 482nd BG – thereafter, pathfinder duties in the 1st BD were taken over by the 305th BG. Altogether, the Eighth Air Force dropped 4800 tons of high explosive on Berlin in five raids during March 1944. Poor weather then returned to save the city from further poundings, leaving the 'heavies' to turn their attention to flying shallow penetration missions against V1 sites in the Pas de Calais.

During April overall command of the Combined Bomber Offensive, and the Eighth Air Force as a whole, officially passed to the newly-appointed Supreme Allied Commander, Gen Dwight D Eisenhower.

MORE WEATHER WORRIES

Any new Eighth Air Force offensive was curtailed by the weather, and it was not until 8 April that the 'heavies' were able to assemble in force when 639 bombers were sent to bomb a series of aircraft depots throughout western Germany – 34 aircraft failed to return. The following day (Easter Sunday) saw the 1st BD assigned the Fw 190 plant and airfield at Marienburg. Only 98 B-17s actually reached the target, and no fighter support was available because of bad weather and the distance involved to the site. No diversionary missions were flown either. Altogether, the day's missions to Germany and Poland cost the Eighth Air Force 32 bombers.

On the 10th 730 'heavies' attacked airfield targets in France and the Low Countries, whilst on the 11th 900+ bombers hit six Junkers and

B-17Gs of the 91st BG taxy out at Bassingbourn. The two nearest Fortresses are olive drab B-17G-25-BO 42-31678 *LITTLE PATCHES* and B-17G-25-VE 42-97636, both from the 324th BS. Two visiting 78th FG P-47Ds (at right) and a natural-metal P-51D can also be seen. *LITTLE PATCHES* made an emergency landing at Raydon fighter airfield on 3 November 1944, and later transferred to the 401st BS, before being returned to the USA on 8 June 1945. 42-97636 'did the groups', for after being assigned to the 91st BG on 27 April 1944, it was reassigned to the 351st BG on 14 June 1944, the 305th BG on 7 August and, finally, the 401st BG on 26 August. The bomber was transferred to the Ninth Air Force postwar, and was salvaged in Germany in April 1946 (*USAF via Tom Cushing*)

B-17G-45-BO 42-97315 of the 532nd BS/381st BG burns in a field near Halstead, in Essex on 5 May 1944 after two engines caught fire during a test run. Capt Douglas Winters and his three crew all escaped without serious injury (*via Mike Bailey*)

Focke-Wulf assembly plants in eastern Germany. Eighty-eight Fortresses from the 1st BD were assigned factories at Cottbus and Sorau, whilst the 92nd BG bombed the industrial area in the city of Stettin. The group lost six B-17s (all from the 325th BS), which fell victim to a combination of vicious and persistent attacks by fighters – Bf 110s from ZG 26 in particular – and a concentrated flak barrage over the target.

The 305th BG was also part of the 40th CBW formation sent to bomb Stettin, and during the course of the mission an outstanding act of bravery resulted in yet another bomber crewman receiving America's highest award for bravery – the second Medal of Honor bestowed upon a member of the group. A pilot in the 364th BS, 1Lt Edward S Michael, aided by co-pilot 2Lt Franklin Westberg, succeeded in bringing the badly shot up B-17G 42-38131 *Bertie Lee* home to England after it had been devastated by cannon fire over the target. Despite both pilots being badly wounded (along with were several other members of the crew), they pulled the Fortress out of a 3000 ft dive, before ordering most of the crew to bale out. It was then that the wounded bombardier found that his parachute had been damaged, forcing him to stay aboard the B-17.

Michael then decided to attempt to fly the aircraft back to England, and after dodging enemy fighters over Germany, he descended to low altitude in order to avoid the attention of flak batteries. Barely airworthy, the bomber was somehow coaxed back across the North Sea, where an extremely weak Michael successfully crash-landed the B-17 at an RAF airfield near Grimsby – despite his undercarriage and flaps having been put out of operation and the ball turret being stuck in the lowered position, with its guns pointing downwards! The airspeed indicator was also inoperable, and the bomb-bay doors were jammed fully open. Michael's miraculous feat had saved the bombardier's life, and he became the second member of the 364th BS to receive the Medal of Honor.

Bad weather on 12 April saw the 'heavies' sent to bomb aircraft plants in central Germany forced to turn back early, although by the following day conditions had improved enough to allow the 1st BD to hit the ball-bearing plants at Schweinfurt for the third time. The leader of the division on this day was 379th BG CO, Col (later general) Maurice 'Mo' Preston. Flying at the head of the leading 41st CBW, his aircraft encountered strong fighter opposition, as he later recounted years after the war;

'The great majority of attacks were concentrated on a single box – a single element of the wing formation. In this case it was the high box rather than the low box, which was normally attacked. Presumably, the high box (384th BG) was chosen because it was separated some distance from the remaining boxes. I made a determined effort via the radio to induce the element leader to get back into formation, but to no avail. In any event, the top element leader failed to comply with

B-17G-50-BO 42-102496 *SPECIAL DELIVERY* of the 359th BS/303rd BG on 25 May 1944. This 'Fort' crash-landed at Molesworth on 18 September 1944 and was salvaged (*USAF via Robert M Foose*)

B-17G-30-DL 42-38113 was the 1000th Fortress built by the Douglas Aircraft Company (altogether, Douglas built 2395 G-models) at Long Beach, California. Assigned to the 750th BS/457th BG and named *Rene III* in honour of CO Col James R Luper's wife. On 27 May 1944 Luper led the 'Fireball Outfit', and the 1st BD, to Ludwigshafen in *Rene III*. The flak was heavy and fighters made head-on attacks that verged on the suicidal. The bomber was badly shot up, but Luper managed to nurse her back to a crash-landing at Glatton, where the B-17 was repaired to fly again. Three other Fortresses in the 457th failed to return, and a further 19 were severely mauled. On 7 October Luper led the 457th BG to Politz, whereupon *Rene III* was hit in two engines, which burst into flames. The fires quickly spread, engulfing the starboard wing and causing the outboard engine to fall away. Seven crew, including Luper, jumped from the doomed B-17, which crashed in Stettin Bay, its bombload exploding on impact – Luper became a PoW. Having survived World War 2, Luper was subsequently killed in a B-26 crash in February 1953 while serving as deputy inspector general for security at Strategic Air Command (*Douglas*)

my orders (whether or not he received them is something else), but it could perhaps be said that he paid dearly for it – he and his entire formation. Every single aircraft (eight B-17Gs) in that formation was shot down on that single pass made by the German fighters. I never saw such a thing before or since. One pass – scratch one entire formation!'

Thereafter, the weather intervened, providing a much needed respite for weary crews. On 22 April the air echelon of the 398th BG, led by its CO, Col Frank P Hunter, landed at Nuthampstead (Station 131), in Hertfordshire, to join the 1st CBW. In their wake came Fortresses at the rate of ten a day, until the group had received its full complement of bombers. While the new crews began their ETO indoctrination lectures, 750 bombers were assembled on 24 April for another mission to the aircraft plants in the Munich area.

The 41st CBW, which bombed the Dornier repair and assembly plants 15 miles south of Munich, was the worst hit during the mission, its formation being attacked by an estimated 200 enemy fighters. The 384th BG experienced the greatest casualties, suffering seven of the wing's 15 losses. The *Jagdwaffe* then moved on to the 40th CBW, whose 92nd BG lost five bombers.

By the end of April 1944 no fewer than 361 heavy bombers had been lost in action during a month of sustained operations over Occupied Europe. Fortunately for the men of the Eighth Air Force, this figure would never be exceeded.

NEW TARGETS

May Day marked the beginning of a series of all-out raids on the enemy's railway network in support of the *Pointblank* Directive. On the 1st 328 'heavies' bombed marshalling yards and railway centres in France and Belgium, but the offensive failed to gain momentum when bad weather over the continent halted deep penetration missions. The Eighth Air Force continued the *Pointblank* raids on the 6th, with the 398th BG making its combat debut on this date. The following two days saw the AAF target Berlin.

On 7 May 549 B-17s bombed the German capital on a day in which over 900 Eighth Air Force 'heavies' attacked targets across western Europe. This was only the second time that more than 1000 'heavies' were airborne on a single day. The following morning 378 B-17s bombed Berlin again, whilst a further 287 B-24s and 49 B-17s raided Brunswick. In the afternoon 80+ Fortresses carried out attacks on targets in France. On the 9th the AAF maintained the pressure on the Germans by sending 797 bombers to hit a variety of enemy airfields and transportation targets in France and the Low Countries.

The Eighth was stood down for 24 hours on the 10th, before despatching 973 'heavies' to bomb marshalling yards in Germany and the Low Countries. On the 12th it was the turn of synthetic oil refineries in the Leipzig area to feel the force of the massed bomb groups of the 1st BD. The following day 689 bombers – again from the 1st BD – hit more oil refineries in Politz, on the Baltic coast. Twelve aircraft failed to return from the mission.

On 14 May the weather grounded all three divisions, and for a further five days missions were scrubbed. When they resumed on the 20th, the Eighth bombed targets in France. Bomb groups were largely stood down on the 21st, and when more bad weather ruled out French targets the following morning, 269 B-17s bombed the shipyards in Kiel instead, whilst a further 23 Fortresses released their bombs prematurely in the same area.

'Big B' was attacked once more on 24 May, some 447 B-17s hitting several designated sites while another 72 struck targets of opportunity in the area. The Luftwaffe was again present in force, and the fighters and flak inflicted 33 losses on the Fortress groups. The hardest hit of all was the 381st BG, which became separated from other groups in the 1st CBW by cloud and thick contrails – eight Fortresses were shot down by the enemy fighters.

In the wake of such a difficult mission to Berlin, crews correctly anticipated a 'milk run' to the Low Countries for the following day. Despite perfect weather, some Fortresses in the 401st BG bombed using radar, for Eighth Air Force HQ needed to know how successful PFF methods could be on D-Day if targets were obscured by cloud. It all served to increase speculation that the invasion of 'Festung Europa' was imminent.

On 27 May the German rail network was attacked again, whilst 24 hours later the Eighth despatched a record 1282 bombers to hit seven oil targets in Germany. The Luftwaffe concentrated their attacks on the leading wings of the formation, in this instance comprising groups from the 1st and 3rd BDs. The escorting fighters were overwhelmed, and the 94th CBW, at the head of the 1st BD, was assailed by over 300 fighters. Altogether, 12 B-17s were lost, including seven from the 401st BG. On the

B-17G-35-BO 42-32076 was named *"SHOO SHOO Baby"* by Lt Paul G McDuffee's crew of the 401st BS/91st BG after the song made famous by The Andrews Sisters, among others. McDuffee's crew flew their first mission (to Frankfurt) in this aircraft on 24 March 1944 the B-17 going on to complete a further 24 combat sorties, during which it was damaged by flak on seven occasions. *"SHOO SHOO SHOO Baby"*, as it was subsequently appended, flew its last mission on 29 May 1944, when engine problems during the raid on Posnan, in Poland, forced Lt Robert J Guenther's crew to head for neutral Sweden. The Swedish government was officially given the B-17 as a gift, and in exchange, American crews were repatriated. *"SHOO SHOO SHOO Baby"* eventually became one of seven B-17s converted by the Swedes to commercial transport configuration. In July 1978 the bomber began a ten-year restoration to flying condition, and on 13 October 1988 was flown to the USAF Museum at Wright-Patterson AFB, Dayton, Ohio, where it is now on permanent display (*USAF*)

B-17Gs in the high and low squadrons of the 303rd BG drop their bombs (*USAF*)

29th 881 bombers returned to the oil refineries at Politz, as well as three Fw 190 factories in north-western Germany – 34 'heavies' were lost.

By now 'invasion fever' was spreading throughout East Anglia, and preparations were put in hand at the myriad American air bases. Training, especially of new crews (and PFF crews), was stepped up. Beginning on 30 May, AAF and RAF bombers made all-out attacks on the French invasion coast. On 5 June the Eighth went to the Pas de Calais, this raid being similar to the many sorties flown by the various groups over the preceding week. In its wake, all sorts of rumours began to persist about an imminent invasion of the enemy coast, and that night wave after wave of RAF aircraft, some towing gliders, flew overhead. American crews knew they would be going over in the morning.

B-17E 41-9100, better known as *Birmingham Blitzkrieg*, first operated with the 414th BS/97th BG from 11 April 1942. One of the 12 Fortresses which flew the first VIII BC mission on 17 August, 41-9100 transferred to the CCRC at Bovingdon on 24 August 1942. In the summer of 1944 the bomber was assigned to the 525th BS/379th BG where, painted with broad white stripes, it was used for target towing and other duties. 41-9100 was salvaged on 18 June 1945 (*via Mike Bailey*)

FINAL VICTORY

At pre-dawn briefings held across southern England in the early hours of 6 June 1944, combat crews learned what their targets on this memorable day would be. At all bases a telegram from Gen Doolittle was read out. The Eighth was required to fly three missions. The first was primarily concerned with neutralising enemy coastal defences and frontline troops, whilst subsequent missions would be directed against lines of communication leading to the beachhead. The bombers would be in good company, with no less than 36 squadrons of P-51s and P-47s patrolling the area. Finally, a message from Gen Dwight D Eisenhower, the Supreme Allied Commander, was relayed to the men.

Briefings over, each group got airborne and headed for the French coast. In the English Channel, through breaks in the cloud, crews spotted ships and boats of all sizes dotting the water as far as the eye could see. Groups in the First Task Force of the 1st BD struck targets in the Cherbourg Peninsular, their bombs being dropped just minutes before the Allied troops hit the beaches. However, the weather soon deteriorated, and not all the Fortress groups were able to fly their second mission of the day.

Altogether, 1361 'heavies' were despatched on the first mission of D-Day, and of these, 1015 dropped their bombs. A total of 528 aircraft were launched on the second mission, but total cloud cover resulted in most of these aircraft returning with their bombloads intact. The third and fourth missions saw 609 bombers successfully deliver their bombs on the designated targets. In all, 1729 'heavies' dropped 3596 tons of bombs on D-Day. No Fortresses were lost.

As the bombers helped to consolidate the beachhead with follow-up strikes on communication targets, the Luftwaffe – their main protagonists – remained conspicuous by their absence. On 7 June further missions were again completed without aerial opposition, as 2Lt Richard R 'Dick' Johnson, co-pilot on the crew of 2Lt Theodore R 'Bud' Beiser in *Buzz Blond* of the 427th BS/303rd BG, confirms;

'We were over enemy territory for 40 minutes, but saw no flak or German fighters. We saw a few friendly fighters above the clouds that were our escorts. We could only get occasional glimpses of the invasion activity. Each of the 18 B-17s of our group were loaded with six 1000-lb bombs to be delivered to a road junction near the invasion coast, close to Condé-sur-Noireau in western France. Eighteen other B-

The mixture of stunned, excited and, above all, elated reactions on the faces of these combat crews in the 306th BG briefing room at Thurleigh on D-Day, 6 June 1944, was repeated at every base in eastern England (*Richards Collection*)

B-17G-35-DL 42-107027 *HIKIN' FOR HOME* **of the 322nd BS/91st BG is seen on a practice mission on 18 June 1944 (***USAF via Mike Bailey***)**

17s from our field were loaded with 500-lb bombs, which were dropped on a road and railroad junction near Flers.

'Our *Buzz Blond* was assigned position No 3 in the 427th BS. This was just behind and to the left of the lead plane of our squadron, which was called "*SHOO SHOO BABY*" after the song by the Andrews Sisters. The 360th's lead plane was named *Sack Time* after our favourite indoor sport. Lead plane of the 358th BS was *Princess Pat*, with the usual seductive nose-art. Two of our aircraft failed to bomb because of malfunctions. Due to overcast at the target, we bombed by radar from an average altitude of 21,000 ft.'

Tactical targets in France continued to be attacked until 15 June, when the 1st BD switched to bombing targets in northern France – mostly airfields, which could be used to launch Luftwaffe attacks on the Normandy beachhead. During such raids on Le Bourget and Melum, near Paris, on 14 June, five B-17s in the 457th BG, including the lead ship carrying Col Cobb from the 94th CBW (flown by 2Lt Malcolm E Johnson), were brought down by flak. One of the bombers successfully ditched in the Channel, although five of its crew drowned before ASR could reach them.

A badly wounded gunner from the 379th BG has his wounds treated at Kimbolton following the mission to Bremen on 24 June 1944 (*Richards Collection***)**

V1 sites in the Pas de Calais continued to be bombed throughout this period, and supply drops were also made to the French Resistance movement.

The length of a frontline tour for aircrew had by now been raised from 30 to 35 missions, and it was announced in June that deep penetration sorties would rank equally with short haul raids in the table of missions per tour.

On 20 June a record 1402 'heavies' were sent to bomb oil targets, and in July a series of missions to Germany struck at a variety of key industrial sites. Munich was singled

out for special treatment, missions being flown against the city on three successive days beginning 11 July.

Six days later the 303rd BG's Dick Johnson flew his first mission as first pilot when he participated in a raid on a railway bridge near Peronne, in France;

'1Lt H C Clark was the first new combat pilot to benefit from my status as a veteran combat pilot. The rest of his crew was with me in a new B-17G with the tail number 43-37666, named *Full House* – three sixes and two threes. This airplane would later be involved in a mid-air collision with another unnamed 427th BS B-17 on 9 November 1944, killing 17 men in the two airplanes, and leaving just one survivor. The tail gunner in the other plane escaped when the tail was severed from the fuselage.

'For the 17 July mission each B-17 was carrying two one-ton bombs under the belly of the plane. Our group dropped 71 of these big bombs over the bridge. One bomb from the plane I was flying refused to release, and so we brought it back to Molesworth. It was just as well, since the other 71 bombs missed the bridge despite clear weather.

'Just after I finished my "new Crew" duty in less than a month, on 15 August Lt Clark's B-17, and eight others, were shot down on the mission to Wiesbaden airfield when the 303rd was attacked by 20-30 enemy fighters. Clark and five others within the crew were killed. The *Flying Bison* returned so badly shot up that no attempt was ever made to repair it. I was saddened that my new friends were killed for such a small return on their bombing investment – the airfield was damaged, but not to the extent that the Germans could not repair it quickly.'

B-17G-45-DL 44-6163 *Passaic Warrior* was assigned to the 534th BS/381st BG on 28 June 1944. It completed over 71 combat missions, and was flown to Kingman, Arizona, for scrapping in November 1945 (*USAF*)

FINAL VICTORY

87

B-17G-50-BO 42-102453 *PRINCESS PAT* of the 358th BS/303rd BG, nosed over at Molesworth on 25 July 1944 when it was being flown by 2Lt O B Larson. The chin turret stoved in and three of the propeller units suffered shock damage, but no-one was seriously injured (*USAF via Robert M Foose*)

On 18 July the principal German research and development centre at Peenemünde, on the Baltic coast, was bombed. The MPI was well covered with bomb hits, and smoke was reported rising to 12,000 ft. The raid prompted accolades from Gen Spaatz, among others, who described it as 'one of the finest examples of precision bombing I have seen'. One of his staff officers, Gen Williams, also added, 'On this vital operation the 1st BD again demonstrated its ability to destroy the assigned objective regardless of its location or enemy opposition'.

Peenemünde was the furthest penetration raid into north-east Germany ever flown by AAF 'heavies', and it was not until after the war that the site's importance was fully realised by the Allies.

On 19 July some 1200 bombers attacked targets in south-central Germany again. Two days later the Eighth returned to Schweinfurt. Budd Peaslee's 1st Scouting Force of Mustangs and Mosquitoes, which had first been used on the 16 July mission to Munich, were instrumental in preventing the 1st BD entering a cloud belt which towered to 28,000 ft. Peaslee's scouting force flew just ahead of the main bombing formation, transmitting up-to-the-minute weather reports back to the task force commander to prevent him leading his bombers into heavy weather fronts which could disrupt the mission and, in some instances, lead to its cancellation. The 1st BD lost only three bombers. The 2nd (which lost an alarming 26 B-24s on the raid) and 3rd BDs wasted no further time in forming their own scouting units.

During July Eighth Air Force bombers also flew seven tactical missions in support of the Allied armies in northern France. On the 24th and 25th, the largest formation of bombers since D-Day dropped thousands of fragmentation bombs and 100-lb GP bombs on German positions in the St Lo area, just ahead of advancing troops of the US First Army. Accuracy was essential, and many bombers returned with their bomb loads intact, rather than risk dropping them on their own troops. The aerial armada paved the way for the breakout, and several days later Allied and German troops clashed in the Battle of Brittany.

August followed the same operational pattern as July, with bombing raids on airfields in France and strategic targets in Germany. On the 1st bomb groups struck at airfields in France, whilst on the 5th the AAF returned to strategic targets, with all-out raids against 11 separate centres in central Germany. Next day the B-17s attacked Berlin, as well as oil and manufacturing centres in other cities. From 19 to 24 August a low pressure system gathered over the British Isles and western Europe, preventing any missions being flown. During the five days of stand down, it was announced that Paris had been liberated, and it was also reported that the Rumanians wished to seek peace. It seemed the war would be over by Christmas.

On 11 September – the date of the second *Frantic* shuttle-bombing mission from England to Russia – an estimated 525 enemy fighters attacked the Eighth Air Force's bomber formations, shooting down most of the 52 'heavies' that were lost. One of these was *Canvas Back IV* of the 326th BS/92nd BG, flown by 1Lt John E Glasco Jr, which was deputy group lead for the attack on Merseburg. Engineer-gunner T/Sgt Ernest M Heidt recalls;

'All went well until we passed the IP and were on the bomb run. The bomb-bay doors were open, and at approximately one minute from "Bombs Away" at 29,000 ft, we took a direct hit which took off about five-foot of the left wing tip and part of the aileron. We immediately drifted towards the lead ship, so Glasco dove. Then we went into a flat spin and salvoed our bombs. While in the flat spin we took a direct hit in the ball turret area, which blew the ball gunner and radio gunner out of the plane. I dropped to the floor and groped for my chest pack 'chute and headed for the forward escape hatch. Glasco was alone fighting the controls with his feet on the instrument panel. I shouted at him if I could help. He shouted back, "Get the Hell Out!"'

Somehow Glasco survived, as did five other members of his crew, but the navigator, ball gunner and tail gunner were all killed. *Canvas Back IV* was the first B-17 to go down over Merseburg, and by the time enemy fighters had intercepted the remainder of the 92nd BG after they had passed over the target, a further 13 Fortresses had been lost. Pilot Jack Sargeant, who was flying a B-17 in the low squadron, had a close shave;

'While on the bomb run, for some reason the co-pilot and I noticed that the outside air temperature was -60°C. This was probably the reason why the flight deck interior was covered with about an inch of hoar frost. The second surprise came just after "Bombs Away", when another outfit came towards us at the same altitude on a westerly course. This proved more than a little unnerving. Needless to say, the flak was going pretty good at this time. At "Bombs Away" I heard the bombardier say, "Bombs . . ." At that precise moment we took a

B-17G-45-DL 44-6158 from the 327th BS/92nd BG at RAF Woodbridge, suffered terrible flak damage during the raid on Merseburg on 13 September 1944. Piloted by 1Lt Elvan E Hendrickson, the bomber received a direct flak hit which killed T/Sgt William B Post, radio operator, and S/Sgts Robert L Shackelford, ball turret gunner, and Frank Wililewski, waist gunner. Despite this, the bomber's surviving crewmen managed to return safely to base, although four other Fortresses from the group were not so lucky. One of the aircraft lost was B-17G-85-BO 43-38389 *U'V'ad It*, which was the lead bomber for the mission. Flown by 1Lt Howard C Donlon, the aircraft received a direct flak hit ten miles east of the target and exploded. Only two crew survived to be made PoW (*via Truett Woodall*)

pretty good flak hit in the nose area. The co-pilot and I already had our steel helmets on, and when the hit occurred, we ducked toward the middle of the flightdeck. So precise were we that we banged our heads together! The resulting clang was pronounced. Additionally, the hit in the nose caused a loosening of the hoar frost in the cockpit. For a second it looked like a real winter snow storm.

'Naturally, the first thing was to get a damage report from the crew. All reports from the rear were negative, but we knew we had been hit. Finally, we located the damage: the glass dome used by the navigator, George Nobel, had been half shot away. Upon return to base, some groundcrew members took what was left of the glass dome and made it into an ideal wind wing for a jeep. For several months thereafter, whenever I saw that jeep it brought back memories of the Merseburg mission.'

On 27 September the 92nd BG flew its 200th mission when they participated in a raid on the marshalling yards at Cologne. The group was led for the first time by Lt Col James W Wilson, who had assumed command from Col William Reid, who was still suffering from a serious flak wound inflicted during a mission to Gelsenkirchen on 26 August. Twenty-four

B-17G-20-BO 42-31614 *Minnie The Mermaid* was assigned to the 533rd BS/381st BG on 22 January 1944. On 26 November 1944 42-31614 and Lt Nelson's crew failed to return from Merseburg when they force-landed down on the continent. *'The Mermaid* was salvaged on 27 January 1945 (*via Mike Bailey*)

B-17G-35-DL 42-107100 *Century Note* was assigned to the 532nd BS/381st BG at Ridgewell on 6 April 1944. On 16 December it force-landed on the continent, but later returned to Ridgewell to complete more than 47 missions by war's end. *Century Note* was scrapped in Kingman, Arizona, in November 1945 (*USAF*)

B-17G-50-BO 42-102490 *WICKED WITCH* was assigned to the 323rd BS/91st BG on 22 April 1944. On its 70th mission on 20 February 1945, whilst being flown by 1Lt Eddie R McKnight's crew, it suffered a direct flak burst over Nürnberg, in Germany. The pilots' compartment was hit and an explosion was observed, with fire coming from the right side. A flash was also seen emanating from the bomb-bay. The aircraft was last spotted at 10,000 ft, approximately 25 km south of Nürnberg/Fürth. McKnight and five of his crew were killed in action, with the remaining three being made PoW (*via Robert M Foose*)

hours after the Cologne raid, the Luftwaffe succeeded in penetrating a strong force of American fighter escorts to shoot down 11 Fortresses from the 303rd BG en route to Magdeburg.

EFFECTIVE BOMBING

Despite mounting losses, there was increasing evidence that the Eighth's bombing offensive – against oil targets in particular – was reaping rewards. Doolittle continued to apply pressure on the German oil-manufacturing industry. On 7 October the 1st BD was sent to the refineries at Politz once again. The 457th BG was led by group CO, Col James R Luper, in *Rene III*.

Also onboard were Group Surgeon, Maj Gordon Haggard, Group Navigator, Capt Norman Kriehn and Group Bombardier, Capt Henry Loades. Heavy flak at the target hit *Rene III* in two engines, setting them on fire. The bomb-bay doors were immediately closed, and although Luper managed to keep the crippled bomber level for a few moments, the fire spread, engulfing the starboard wing and causing the outboard engine to fall away. At this point Luper, and six others, jumped from the doomed B-17, which still contained its full bomb load. *Rene III* subsequently exploded upon impact. One man who baled out of the waist hatch had his parachute on fire as it fluttered open, and he was soon engulfed in flames. Only Luper and Kriehn survived being shot down to become PoWs.

Three more B-17s from the 457th BG were lost over the target, including Luper's wingman, and the deputy lead ship, flown by 2Lt Vernon M Moland. Thirty-eight aircraft that returned to Glatton were all badly damaged, and 16 B-17s required sub-depot repairs – only four bombers had come through unscathed. A short time later Col Harris E Rogner assumed command of the 'Fireball Outfit'.

During October 1944 many combat-seasoned personnel within the well-established groups returned to the USA after completing their tours. Bad weather during this month also slowed down the Allies' advance all along the western front, and severely hampered bombing missions as well. When the 'heavies' did manage to get airborne, they continued to pound oil-related targets.

One such raid took place on 2 November when the huge I G Farben Industrie's synthetic oil refinery at Leuna, three miles south of Merseburg, was bombed. At the pre-mission briefing, crews were warned that German fuel and replacement pilots were in such short supply that Reichsmarschall Göring was massing his forces to strike a telling blow on a single mission in a last ditch effort to end the daylight bombing campaign. All the embattled *Jagdwaffe* needed was the opportunity to catch a formation of bombers unescorted, and on the 2nd the 457th BG proved to be the unlucky group.

B-17Gs of the 91st BG head for their target. The nearest aircraft is B-17G-35-BO 42-32095 *ACK-ACK ANNIE* from the 322nd BS, which had joined the 91st BG on 16 March 1944 after flying with the 457th BG at Glatton. 42-32095 was scrapped at Kingman in 1946
(*USAF via Tom Cushing*)

B-17G-80-BO 43-38172 of the 601st BS/398th BG, piloted by 1Lt Lawrence De Lancey, made it back to Nuthampstead from Cologne on 15 October 1944 after losing its nose, and the bombardier, to a direct flak hit over Cologne (*USAF*)

Blown 35 miles off course by 50-knot winds en route to Merseburg, 35 aircraft from the 'Fireball Outfit' headed for the secondary target at Bernberg instead. They were greeted by more than 400 fighters. Attacks were initially made on the low squadron from six to eight o'clock low by 40 Fw 190s. Despite being totally out-gunned, the bombers did their best to fend off their assailants, but one by one the B-17s fell out of formation and hurtled earthward. *Lady Margaret*, piloted by Lt William J Murdock Jr, had its fin severed by the wing of a passing Fw 190, whilst several other hits ensured that it went down in flames. Six crew survived to become PoWs. *Prop Wash*, with Lt Gordon E Gallagher at the controls, followed soon after.

A further seven B-17s had exploded or crashed, with a further nine badly shot up, by the time escorting P-51s eventually arrived on the scene. Losses throughout the 1st BD were so bad on this mission (the 91st BG lost no fewer than 12 Fortresses) that groups were stood down for two days following the raid.

No matter how stiff the opposition, or the number of casualties suffered, AAF bomber crews were noted for their press-on-regardless spirit, and none more so than the 92nd BG's 1Lt Cyrus R Broman, pilot of B-17G *Hubert*. On 6 November, during a mission to Hamburg, Broman lost the turbo-supercharger on the No 1 engine of his bomber at 27,500 ft while climbing to attain bombing altitude. By applying full boost to the other three engines, he managed to maintain formation for a short while until the propeller on the No 3 engine ran away. Unable to keep up on two good engines, Broman decided to descend in order to gain flying speed, and he arrived at the target as scheduled.

Although the rest of his formation had reached, and bombed, the target, by now, Broman continued and dropped his bombs too. At this point fire knocked out the oxygen system of co-pilot, 2Lt Walter Woodrow, and forced Broman to dive rapidly so that the co-pilot could breathe. Although now well within range of flak batteries, *Hubert* returned safely to Podington, where Broman duly received the DFC for his efforts.

On 9 November the 'heavies' returned to tactical missions in support of Gen George Patton's Third Army, whose progress had been halted at the fortress city of Metz. Exactly a week later another tactical mission to targets just east of Aachen was flown as the Allied armies continued their advance towards Germany. Again, careful planning was needed in order to avoid casualties to friendly troops. The mission proved to be a great success, although worsening weather conditions encountered during the return leg forced some groups to fly to bases in northern England, where they remained for several days until the weather cleared.

On 21 November the Eighth returned to the hated city of Merseburg, infamous for the flak batteries that ringed it. Four days later the same target was bombed again, although the results from this mission were so poor that the AAF revisited Merseburg's oil refineries for a third time on the 30th. The 1st BD attacked the synthetic plant at Zeitz, while the 3rd BD struck at the city itself, some 20 miles to the north. Both divisions flew the route as briefed as far as Osnabruck, where the leading 1st BD formation flew on instead of turning for Zeitz. The AAF lost 29 'heavies' and more than 40 fighters on this bleak day.

The following month the worst winter weather to strike England in 54 years effectively grounded the Eighth Air Force for days on end. Taking advantage of this, Field Marshal Karl von Rundstedt launched an audacious counter-offensive through the forests of the Ardennes on the 16th. His Panzer columns punched a hole in the American lines to open up a 'bulge' in the Allied frontline.

Still firmly grounded by fog and snow, the bombing force in England was powerless to intervene until 23 December, when 'heavies' attacked road and rail targets in an effort to stem the tide of troops and materials entering the salient. So effective was the 1st BD's attack on the marshalling yards at Ehrang, in Germany, that it earned a commendation from Eighth Air Force 'staffer' Brig Gen Howard M Turner for the 'excellent manner in which the mission was executed'. He went on;

381st BG B-17Gs of the 533rd BS ('VE') and 535th BS ('MS') (USAF)

'Operating in extremely adverse weather conditions, these units exhibited a high degree of determination and skill in clearing the Division area, attacking the marshalling yards at Ehrang and landing in weather conditions equally as adverse without the loss of a single aircraft. Excellent bombing results were obtained. Convey to participating officers and men my appreciation of a job well done.'

On Christmas Eve 1944 the Field Order at all bases called for a maximum effort, and to meet it most groups put up all available aircraft, including 'war wearies' and assembly ships. However, some 3rd BD bases were still congested with 1st BD Fortresses which had landed there after the mission of 23 December due to their own airfields being 'socked in'. Visibility was still poor, and this led to many accidents during take-off. For instance, at Podington 2Lt Robert K Seeber's Fortress crashed into a wood about 200 yards to the left of the runway which had not been visible during the take-off run because of the thick fog. Two minutes later the 327th BS B-17 exploded, killing six of the crew.

At Glatton the 457th managed to get six aircraft off in reduced visibility, but the seventh crashed at the end of the runway and operations were brought to a halt for a time. Despite these accidents the Eighth mounted the largest single attack so far when 2034 'heavies' headed for Germany (almost 1900 actually bombed). The 1st BD made a direct tactical assault on airfields in the Frankfurt area and on lines of communication immediately behind the German 'bulge'. Crews were told that their route was planned on purpose to overfly the ground troops' positions in order to boost their morale.

Hitting a variety of targets, the Christmas Eve raids severely hampered von Rundstedt's lines of communication, although many bombers crashed upon their return to England, where drizzle and overcast played havoc with landing patterns. Tired crews put down where they could.

Another strike was ordered for 26 December, and groundcrews worked around the clock, but it was all in vain. The weather, and the still scattered groups from the Christmas Eve raid, resulted in only 150 aircraft being despatched. The next day wintry conditions were responsible for a succession of crashes during early morning take-offs. Finally, on 30 December the Eighth again attacked lines of communication, and on New Year's Eve the 1st BD kept up the onslaught, while the 3rd BD hit numerous oil-related targets.

B-17Gs of the 1st AD's 401st BG are seen at a wintry Deenthorpe on 12 January 1945. Nearest aircraft is B-17G-80-BO 43-38077 *DUKE'S MIXTURE* from the 615th BS. This aircraft was later re-assigned to the 614th BS, and re-named *Tag A Long*. It finished its days at Kingman in November 1945 (*USAF*)

NEW YEAR

January 1945 marked the Eighth's third year of operations, and at last it seemed as if the end of the war was within reach. The German breakthrough in the Ardennes was on the verge of collapse, and the enemy had no reserves left. There were still signs though that the Luftwaffe, at least, was far from finished. On 1 January – the day the Division prefix 'Bomb' was officially changed to 'Air' – the 1st AD encountered enemy fighters in strength during raids on the tank factory at Kassel, an oil refinery at Magdeburg and marshalling yards at Dillenburg. The Magdeburg force, in particular, came under heavy fighter attack, while the Kassel bombers was badly hit by flak.

The next day the 'heavies' once again pounded lines of communication, and raids of this nature continued for several days until the Allies started to regain the land lost during the opening phase of the 'Battle of the Bulge'. On 5 January the severe wintry weather over England was again responsible for several fatal take-off accidents at the start of a mission to Frankfurt. However, several days of fine weather from the 6th onwards allowed the bombers to complete more support missions for the ground troops, with lines of communication, airfields and marshalling yards being repeatedly hit.

Through the direct intervention of the Eighth Air Force, in conjunction with the Ninth Air Force, the RAF and Allied troops on the ground, the last great German offensive of World War 2 was ultimately stopped. Tactical missions were flown throughout the remainder of January, but when morale began to sag as mission after mission was scrubbed, often just after take-off due to poor weather, the Eighth reverted instead to shallow penetration raids on *Noball* sites in France.

At the Yalta Conference in early February 1945, Soviet leader Josef Stalin, acting on requests from his army chiefs, asked that the RAF and Eighth Air Force paralyse Berlin and Leipzig so as to prevent troops moving from the west to the eastern front. British Prime Minister Winston Churchill and American President Franklin D Roosevelt agreed a series of massive air attacks on the German capital, as well as other cities such as Dresden and Chemnitz. These were not only administrative centres controlling military and civilian movements, but also the main communication hubs through which the bulk of the enemy's war traffic flowed. These cities would be devastated by the attacks which were to come.

Spaatz set the wheels in motion with a raid on Berlin on 3 February, at a time when Marshal Zhukov's Red Army was only 35 miles from the city centre, and the capital was jammed with refugees fleeing from the advancing Soviet forces. The raid was designed to cause as much havoc as possible. Just over 1000 Fortresses were assembled for the mission, and a total of 2267 tons of bombs reigned down into the 'Mitte', or central district of 'Big B'. Reconnaissance photographs later

B-17G-95-BO 43-38832 *Irene* of the 306th BG taxies out from its base in mid-February 1945 with a *Disney* bomb fixed beneath its wing. On 10 February 150 B-17s bombed targets in Holland, and during the mission *Disney* bombs, invented by Capt Edward Terrell RN, were used for the first time. Nine B-17s from the 92nd BG, led by Col James W Wilson, dropped 18 such devices on E-boat pens at Ijmuiden. The 4500-lb bomb was powered by a rocket motor in the tail, and it was designed to pierce 20 ft of concrete before exploding. Their hefty weight prevented carriage in the bomb-bay of a B-17, and so one *Disney* was carried under each wing. A single hit was recorded at the north end of the pens, and further trials were ordered, but the Allies' sweeping victories in the Low Countries, and the vast distance to suitable targets in Norway, brought the *Disney* missions almost to an end. *Irene* was transferred to the 92nd BG on 9 May 1945 (*Richards Collection*)

revealed that an area one-and-a-half miles square, stretching across the southern half of the 'Mitte', had been devastated at a cost of 21 bombers. Another six 'heavies' crash-landed behind Soviet lines.

Of the bombers that returned, 93 had suffered major flak damage. Among the losses was veteran B-17G 42-97678 *The Birmingham Jewel*, which had only recently set an Eighth Air Force record by completing 128 missions with the 526th BS/379th BG.

Magdeburg and Chemnitz were bombed on the 6th, but the most devastating series of raids fell upon the old city of Dresden, in eastern Germany, starting with an 800-bomber mission flown by the RAF on the night of 13 February. Two waves of heavy bombers produced firestorms that inflicted horrendous casualties among the civilian population. The following day, 400 bombers of the Eighth Air Force visited the already burning city, and bombs stoked up the fires created by the RAF.

On 16 February the 'heavies' hit the Hoesch coking plant at Dortmund, which was estimated to be producing 1000 tons of benzol a month. Bombing was completed visually, and again the Luftwaffe was noticeable by its virtual absence.

Twenty-four hours later the Eighth resumed its oil offensive with raids on synthetic refineries at Lutzkendorf and Meresburg. While still over the North Sea bad weather forced all except one 1st AD Fortress to return to England. Altogether, 22 bombers were lost in crash-landings whilst trying to land at their bases in England. The sole B-17 that ignored the recall continued to Essen, where it dropped its bombs, before returning alone without meeting any opposition! Such an occurrence would have been unthinkable just a few months before, but now the Luftwaffe had been effectively grounded through both a lack of pilots and petrol.

On 22 February the Eighth launched Operation *Clarion*, which resulted in the systematic destruction of the German communications

B-17G-70-DL 44-6915 of the 524th BS/379th BG failed to return from a mission on 19 March 1945, when it put down at Brussels. 44-6915 later returned to Kimbolton, surviving the war to finish its days at Kingman in November 1945 (*USAF*)

network. No less than 6000 aircraft from seven different commands were airborne on th is day, and they struck at transportation targets throughout western Germany and northern Holland. All were selected with the object of preventing troops being transported to defend the eastern front, which was now only a few miles from the outskirts of Berlin itself.

Despite the low altitudes flown on this day, only five bombers were lost, including one to an Me 262 jet fighter. On the 23rd just two 'heavies' failed to return from the 1193 despatched.

German flak batteries were now also beginning to feel the affect of the Allied bombing, being deprived of ammunition to the point where gunners were being instructed to conserve their meagre reserves. On 26 February even the normally notorious flak defences of Berlin managed to shoot down just five bombers.

By March 1945 the Third Reich was on the brink of defeat, and the systematic destruction of German oil production plants, airfields and communications centres had virtually driven the Luftwaffe from the skies. Despite fuel and pilot shortages, Me 262s could still be expected to conduct the occasional rare attack, and during March almost all interceptions of American heavy bombers were made by jet fighters. However, they had arrived too late, and in too few numbers, to prevent the inevitable Allied victory.

On 18 March a record 1327 bombers blasted Berlin. Although flak was particularly hazardous on this mission, the principal threat was provided by 37 Me 262s of I. and II./JG (*Jagdverband*) 7. Attacking the massive bomber formation, the jets downed 16 bombers and five fighters (another 16 'heavies' were forced to land inside Soviet territory) for the loss of only two Me 262s. By the end of the month the Eighth had lost 30 bombers to the German twin-engined jets.

The threat posed by the Messerschmitt fighter became such a problem that from 21 March onwards the Eighth flew a series of raids specifically against airfields known to be used by the *Jagdverband*. These missions also coincided with the build up of troops for the impending crossing of the Rhine by Allied forces. On 23/24 March, under a 66-mile long smoke screen, and aided by 1747 bombers of the Eighth Air Force, Field Marshal Bernard Montgomery's 21st Army Group crossed the Rhine in the north, while further south simultaneous crossings were made by Gen Patton's Third Army.

B-17Gs of the 91st BG drop their bombs on Berlin on 26 February 1945. Altogether, 1102 bombers, escorted by 15 fighter groups, struck at three railway stations in the German capital, as well as targets of opportunity that included Eberswalde (*USAF*)

Everywhere the Allies were victorious, but while the enemy kept on fighting, missions continued almost daily, resulting in bomber crews completing tours in record time. Sgt Walter 'Don' O'Hearn, tail gunner on *El Screamo* (of the 427th BS/303rd BG), flown by Lt Denison and Chuck Haynes, recalls that six of his crew finished 30 missions in just 57 days, starting on 27 February and ending on 25 April 1945;

'This was as short a time for 30 missions as I have ever heard of. Our co-pilot was hit by flak over Berlin and lost his foot. He was a great pilot. Three trips to Berlin were plenty for all of us. We always had lots of flak – "black" flak. Our 26th mission, on 10 April, to Oranienburg, almost within sight of Berlin, which was just 40 miles to the south, was the most frightening of them all. Our group was hit by 6-8 Me 262 jet fighters.'

On 13 April the 398th BG from Nuthampstead flew its 188th mission of the war, to Neumunster. Over the target disaster struck when the bombardier in a leading aircraft prematurely salvoed his bombs, causing two of them to touch about 400 ft below the B-17. These devices were fitted with close-proximity RDX fuses, which were most unstable at all times unless handled with great care. The resulting explosion brought down six Fortresses from the 601st BS, five of which had to be abandoned over the continent. Despite the fratricide, bombing results were later described as 'excellent'.

On 17 April Dresden was attacked yet again. By this late stage of the war the German 'corridor' had shrunken so rapidly that the American and Soviet bomb lines now crossed at several points on briefing maps. During the week commencing 18 April, missions were briefed and scrubbed almost simultaneously, until on the 25th the Eighth Air Force flew its final full-scale combat mission of the war, to the Skoda armaments plants at Pilsen, in Czechoslovakia. The 40 aircraft from the 92nd BG that participated in this operation were given the honour of leading the strike force.

Known as 'Fame's Favoured Few', the 92nd was the oldest group in the Eighth, and the Pilsen raid represented its 310th mission of the war. The 303rd BG was also a part of the bombing force on this day, the group's participation taking its tally of missions flown to a record 364. A number of other groups came close to matching the Molesworth 'Hell's Angels'.

With final victory just two weeks away, losses were experienced on this final raid. Lt Lewis B Fisher and his crew became the last in the 92nd to be shot down when their bomber (the 154th lost in action by the group) was struck by a flak burst. It was seen over Pilsen going into the clouds in a spin, trailing flame and black smoke. No parachutes were observed.

Visual bombing was performed on this day, although several runs were deemed necessary because of the cloudy conditions in the target area. The following day the American and Russian armies met at Torgau, and the world waited for the inevitable unconditional surrender. Further bombing missions were cancelled, and the bomb groups were stood down. At Podington on 29 April the long awaited, and once postponed, 300th mission party finally got into full swing. At Kimbolton the 379th BG celebrated the fact that they had flown more sorties (10,492) than any other bomb group in the Eighth Air Force, had dropped more bombs on the enemy than any other group (26,459.6 tons) and had the lowest abort rate of all groups in combat since 1943. The 379th also boasted the

B-17G-30-BO 42-31909 *NINE O NINE* of the 323rd BS/91st BG was named by radio man Jack Grosh, on Lt Art Klinger's crew. He created this sobriquet by using the last three digits of the B-17's serial number. *NINE O NINE* was assigned to the 323rd BS at Bassingbourn on 24 February 1944, and when photographed on 18 June 1945, this famous Fortress had completed no less than 140 combat missions, 126 of them without an abort. This was an Eighth Air Force record. *NINE O NINE* was scrapped at the end of the year (*USAF via Tom Fitton*)

Fortress with the most missions – 524th BS B-17G 42-40003 *'Ol Gappy'* is believed to have flown 157 sorties.

During the final week of the European war the bomb groups made a series of food drops to starving civilians in Holland. Starting on 1 May, Fortress crews began flying mercy missions as part of Operation *Chowhound*. RAF bombers had commenced relief flights (code-named Operation *Manna*) two days earlier. Plywood floors were placed inside the B-17 bomb-bays, rigged to the bomb release shackles. The bomb-bays were then loaded with food packages. Once loaded, the bombers flew to Holland at low altitude and dropped the supplies over airfields marked with white crosses. One of the main drop points was Amsterdam-Schiphol. Many Dutch civilians waved at the 'Forts' during the drops, and pilots in turn waggled their wings in acknowledgement. Altogether, six supply drop missions were flown by the Eighth Air Force up to 5 May.

Within 72 hours, news of the final German surrender was made known to the men of the AAF at bases throughout eastern England. In the immediate wake of victory in Europe B-17 groups were assigned many tasks, such as flying Allied PoWs from their camps in eastern Europe back to France, and transporting displaced persons from Linz, in Austria, to their homes in France, Holland, Denmark and numerous other recently-liberated countries. The B-17 crews also flew troops heading for the CBI on the first leg of their journey from the UK to Casablanca, as well as acting as 'moving vans' for fighter groups that had been posted to Germany as part of the newly-created occupation force. In addition, *Trolley* and *Revival* missions were flown to bombed out cities with B-17s crammed with ground personnel to show them what the devastated cities looked like from the air.

APPENDICES

B-17 BOMB GROUP ASSIGNMENTS

VIII BC/1st BOMB WING/1st BOMB DIVISION/1st AIR DIVISION

Group	Squadrons	Codes	Wing & Command	Assignment
97th BG	340th BS		VIII BC:	20/5/42
	341st BS		1st BW:	8/42
	342nd BS		To 12th AF XII BC:	4/9/42
	414th BS			
301st BG	32nd BS		VIII BC:	20/5/42
	352nd BS		1st BW:	8/42
	353rd BS		To 12th AF XII BC:	14/9/42
	419th BS			
91st BG	322nd BS	(LG)	VIII BC, 1st BW:	9/42
	323rd BS	(OR)	101st PCBW:	2/43
	324th BS	(DF)	1st CBW:	13/9/43
	401st BS	(LL)		
92nd BG	325th BS	(NV)	VIII BC, 1st BW:	8/42
	326th BS	(JW)	102nd PCBW:	5/43
	327th BS	(UX)	40th CBW:	13/9/43
	407th BS	(PY)		
303rd BG	358th BS	(VK)	VIII BC, 1st BW:	10/9/42
	359th BS	(BN)	102nd PCBW:	2/43
	360th BS	(PU)	103rd PCBW:	5/43
	427th BS	(GN)	41st CBW:	13/9/43
305th BG	364th BS	(WF)	VIII BC, 1st BW:	9/42
	365th BS	(XK)	102nd PCBW:	2/43
	366th BS	(KY)	103rd PCBW:	5/43
	422nd BS	(JJ)	41st CBW:	13/9/43
306th BG	367th BS	(GY)	VIII BC, 1st BW:	9/42
	368th BS	(BO)	101st PCBW:	2/43
	369th BS	(WW)	102nd PCBW:	6/43
	423rd BS	(RD)	40th CBW:	13/9/43
351st BG	508th BS	(YB)	101st PCBW:	5/43
	509th BS	(RQ)	1st CBW:	13/9/43
	510th BS	(TU)	92nd CBW:	1/11/43
	511th BS	(DS)	94th CBW:	15/12/43
379th BG	524th BS	(WA)	103rd PCBW:	5/43
	525th BS	(FR)	41st CBW:	13/9/43
	526th BS	(LF)		
	527th BS	(FO)		
381st BG	532nd BS	(??/VE)	101st PCBW	6/43
	533rd BS	(OQ/VP)	1st CBW:	13/9/43
	534th BS	(JZ/GD)		
	535th BS	(PL/MS)		
384th BG	544th BS	(SU)	103rd PCBW:	6/43
	545th BS	(JD)	41st CBW:	13/9/43
	546th BS	(BK)		
	547th BS	(SO)		
398th BG	600th BS	(N8)	1st CBW:	22/4/44
	601st BS	(30)		
	602nd BS	(K8)		
	603rd BS	(N7)		
401st BG	612th BS	(SC)	92nd CBW:	5/43
	613th BS	(IN)	94th CBW:	15/12/43
	614th BS	(IW)		
	615th BS	(IY)		
457th BG	748th BS		94th CBW:	21/1/44
	749th BS			
	750th BS			
	751st BS			
482nd BG	812th BS	(MI)	VIII BC, 1st BD:	8/1/44
	813rd BS	(PC)	VIII AFCC:	14/2/44
	814th BS	(SI)	VIII FC:	1 Oct 44
			1st AD:	1 Jan 45
Night Leaflet Squadron	422nd BS	(JJ)	VIII BC, 1st BD:	10/43
	406th BS	(J6)	1st BD:	1/44
			VIII AFCC:	2/44
			1st AD:	1/1/45
Radio Countermeasures Squadron			1st AD:	1 Jan 45

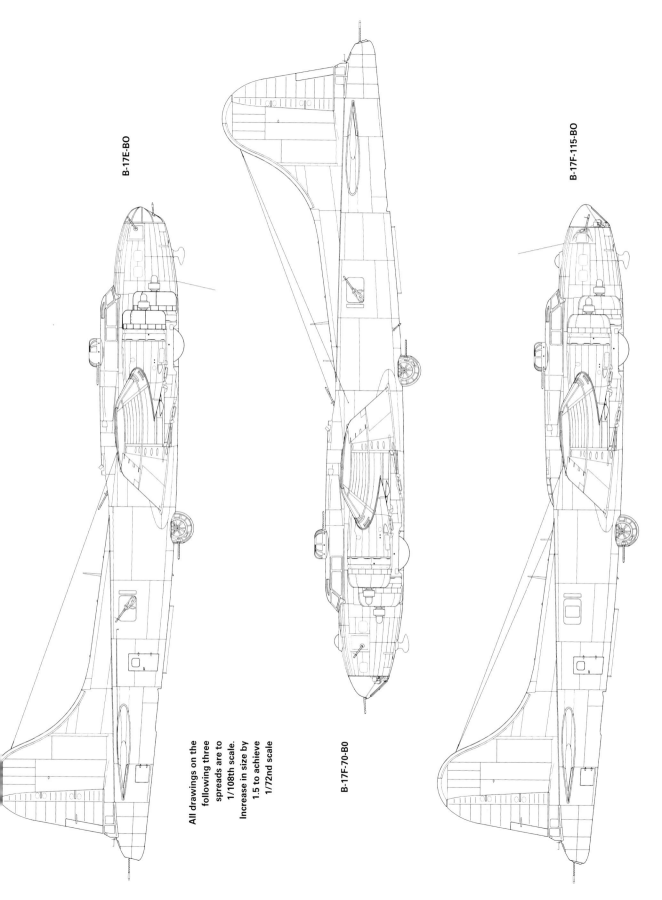

B-17E-BO

B-17F-115-BO

B-17F-70-B0

**All drawings on the
following three
spreads are to
1/108th scale.
Increase in size by
1.5 to achieve
1/72nd scale**

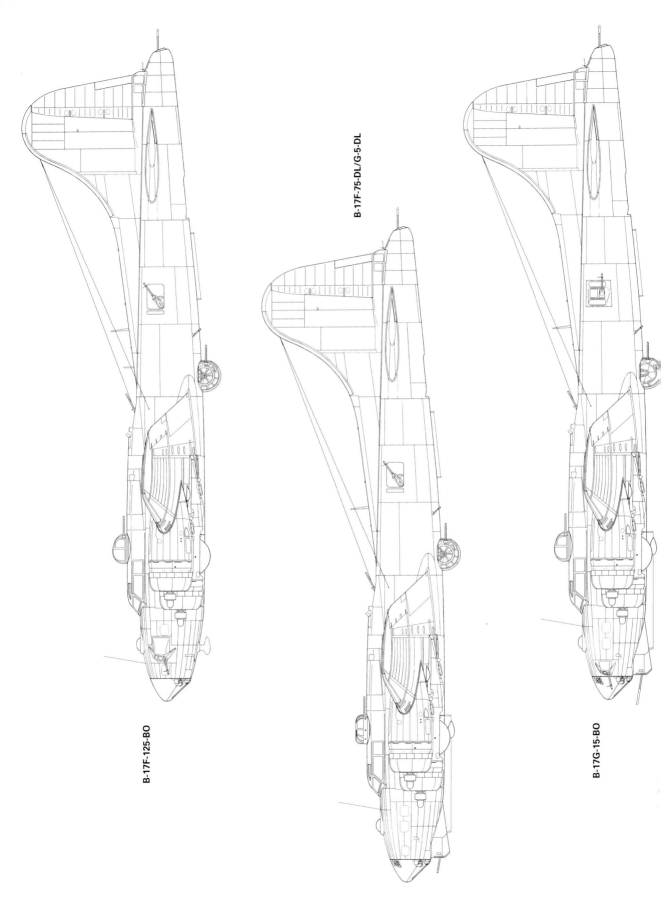

B-17F-75-DL/G-5-DL

B-17F-125-BO

B-17G-15-BO

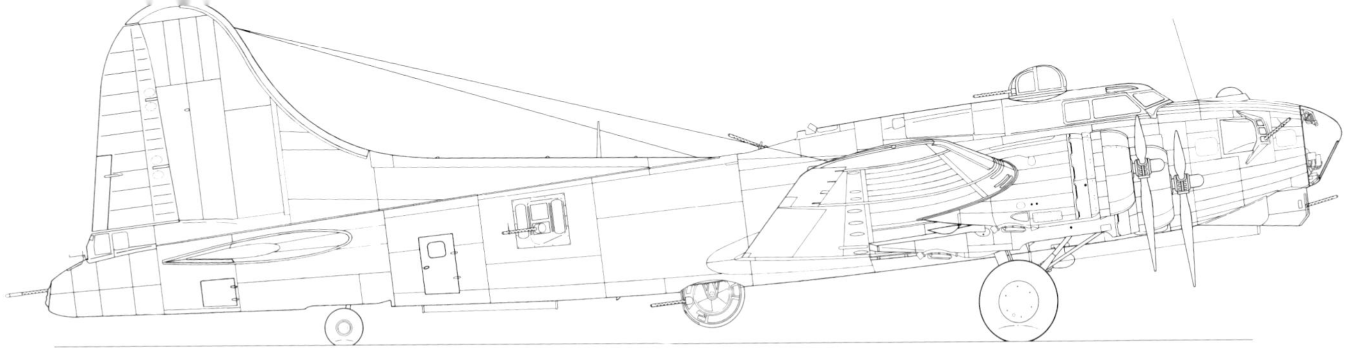

B-17G-30-BO

B-17G-70-BO

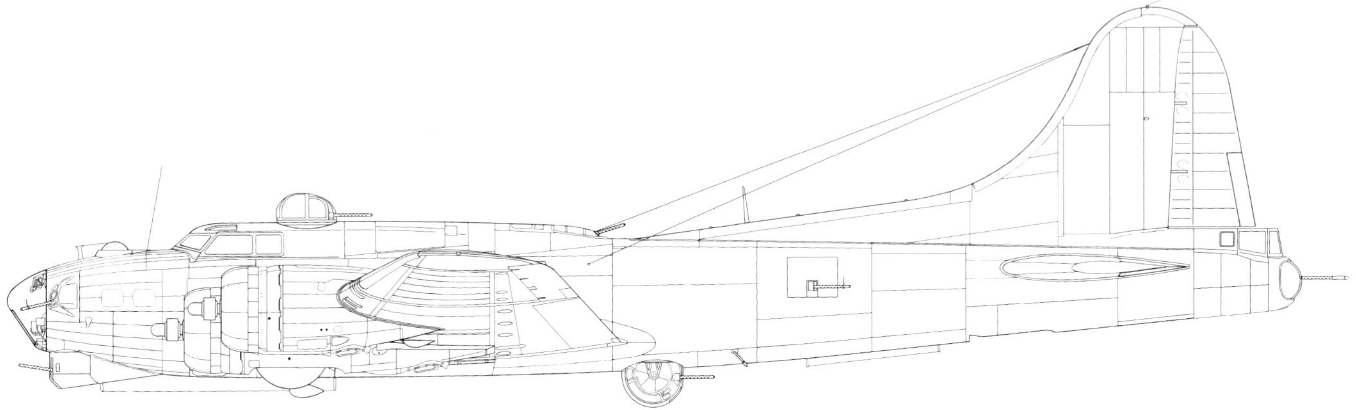

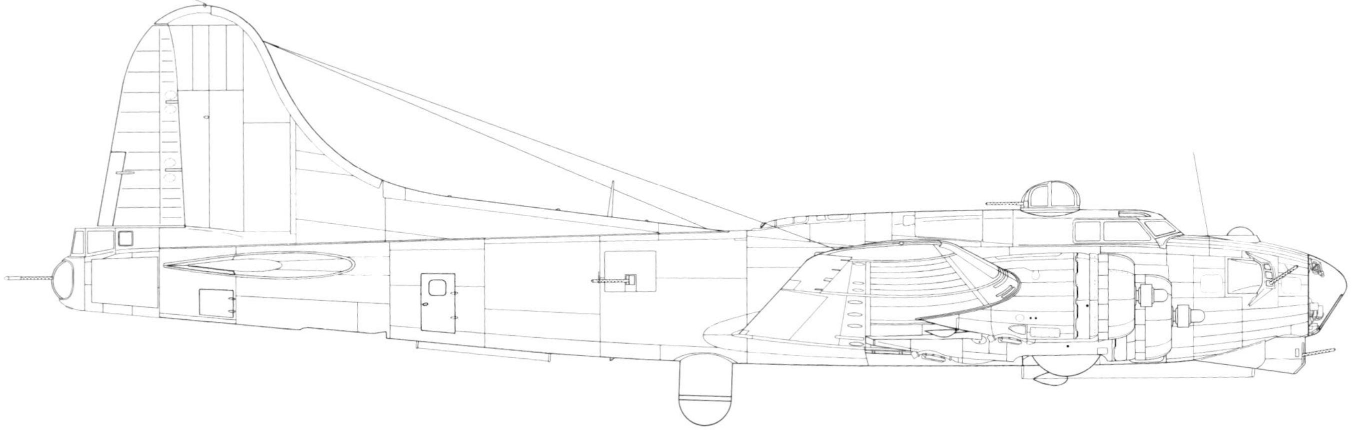

B-17G-50-VE *Mickey Ship*

COLOUR PLATES

General Notes by the Artist

The B-17 was the most modified aircraft to serve with the AAF in World War 2, and as such, most of the aircraft depicted within the colour section do not appear as manufactured. The following commentaries indicate where changes first appear within the series of profiles, which are arranged in order of manufacture. By way of example, the enclosed radio room gun position appears on many of the later profiles, although this was only supposedly introduced with the advent of the B-17G-50-DL and G-55-VE – the last manufactured aircraft to appear within the profiles is a G-50-VE.

Where possible, the colours depicted in the artwork have been matched to original colour photographs. In particular, the olive drab (OD) schemes have been carefully weathered to reflect the length of service of the individual aeroplane featured – OD paint faded in a different way on control surfaces, hence the varying shades on the rudders. Medium green was also used in the early days of VIII BC, and this faded at a slower rate than OD, hence the fact that it stands out considerably more on mixed-camouflage aircraft.

1
B-17E-BO 41-9023 *YANKEE DOODLE* of the 414th BS/97th BG, flown by 1Lt John Dowswell, Polebrook, 17 August 1942
This aircraft was assigned to the 414th BS in March 1942, and arrived at Grafton Underwood in July. Its great claim to fame occurred during the very first VIII BC mission, flown on 17 August 1942, when Brig Gen Ira C Eaker accompanied the bomber's crew to the target at Rouen. Exactly a week later 41-9023 was transferred to the 92nd BG at Bovingdon, before moving once again to the 323rd BS/91st BG on 30 March 1943 – the bomber also flew with the 324th BS during its time with the latter group. Seen here wearing RAF-style camouflage, the *YANKEE DOODLE* boasted identification stripes on the undersurfaces of the wings and stabilisers – red for port and blue for starboard. Note also the word *PUNCH*, painted in yellow, just aft of the tail-mounted twin .50-cal machine guns. Finally, this aircraft features an additional ball-mounted .30-cal machine gun in the nose. 41-9023 survived the carnage in the ETO only to be salvaged (scrapped) on 26 July 1945.

2
B-17E-BO 41-9019 *LITTLE SKUNKFACE* of the 414th BS/97th BG, Polebrook, September 1942
A squadron-mate of *YANKEE DOODLE*, this aircraft was transferred to the 305th BG on 6 November 1942 prior to the 97th BG's move to North Africa. It was subsequently passed on to the 381st BG in June 1943, then operated as a target tug with the 327th BS/92nd BG in July 1943. Just weeks later,

on 27 August, 41-9019 was sent to the 482nd BG at Alconbury, where it remained until it was written off on 21 August 1945. This profile shows the aircraft in its original RAF bomber scheme, although the underside sky blue applied by Boeing at the factory has been painted out with AAF grey. Note also that the pre-war 'U.S. Army' titling is still carried on the wing undersides, despite the repainting.

3
B-17F-15-BO 41-24490 *Jack the Ripper* of the 324th BS/91st BG, flown by Lt William J Crumm, Bassingbourn, November 1942
41-24490 was one of the first aircraft delivered to the 91st BG, being assigned to Lt William J Crumm's crew in the 324th BS on 16 July 1942. They chose the bomber's sinister nickname before they departed for the UK on 27 September. This aircraft subsequently became the only B-17 within the 91st BG to complete the group's first three missions, on 7, 8 and 9 November. Crumm's crew flew this aircraft on 10 of its first 111 missions, before being sent home to share their combat experiences with other crews in training – they prepared a book, titled *Bombing the Nazis*, which was published by the School of Applied Tactics in 1943. A Petty-style pin-up had been added to the right side of the aircraft by this time, *Jack the Ripper* eventually completing a sequence of 26 combat missions before it suffered its first abort. On 22 February 1944 the *'Ripper'* became the last of the original B-17Fs assigned to the 91st BG to be shot down, the aircraft being lost on a raid to Bunde, near Osnabruck in Germany, whilst being flown by 1Lt James Considine. Attacked by enemy fighters, it crashed at Münster, although all bar navigator Henry Schaub succeeded in baling out. This profile reveals that the early B-17F has retained the E-model's Sperry upper turret, which lacks forward glazing. A single .50-cal gun has also been fitted behind the Plexiglas nose, these mountings varying in style. Initially installed 'in the field' in the UK, the additional nose gun was soon part of the combat fitment adopted as standard by modification centres across the USA. This particular aircraft also has an additional sheet of armour plating mounted inside the Plexiglas to give the bombardier added protection against frontal attacks. A further detail unique to the early B-17Fs are the shorter, less rounded, cowlings that were fitted to allow propellers to be feathered more effectively. The name *Suzie Q* appears beneath the co-pilot's window, whilst *Peggy the Georgia Peach* adorns the fuselage centre-section below the waist gunner's window.

4
B-17F-27-BO 41-24561 *THE DUCHESS* of the 359th BS/303rd BG, Molesworth, late summer 1943
This was the aircraft in which lead bombardier 1Lt

Jack Mathis posthumously won the Eighth Air Force's first Medal of Honor during the raid on Vegesack on 18 March 1943 - see chapter 2 for details. One of the original B-17s issued to the 303rd BG at Bangor, Maine, in September 1942, the bomber completed 59 missions with the group prior to being returned to the USA in August 1944 – it was sold for scrap exactly a year later. This profile reveals how the aircraft looked by the late summer of 1943, wearing the revised national insignia that had been instigated in August of that year. Note the word LUCKY painted beneath the pilot's window, along with the playing cards 2 and 5. Like many other B-17s within the 303rd BG, this aircraft also boasted a pin-up on the fin fillet as well as the nose, although in this instance the second female form adorned the starboard side of the vertical surface. Finally, the black rubberised de-icing boots normally worn on the leading edges of the wing and horizontal stabilisers have been removed from this aircraft, exposing the bare metal below.

5

B-17F-27-BO 41-24605 KNOCK-OUT DROPPER of the 359th BS/303rd BG, Molesworth, March 1944

Another 303rd BG 'original', this aircraft became the first Eighth Air Force B-17 to complete 50 combat missions (on 16 November 1943) and 75 combat missions (on 27 March 1944). In order to set the first record, some 12 aborted sorties were tactfully ignored! Initially assigned to Lt Jack Roller's crew during the final phase of their training at Battle Creek, Michigan, they went on to complete 18 missions in KNOCK-OUT DROPPER – including the bomber's 25th operational sortie. Their tour over, Roller and his crew left the aircraft behind at Molesworth and returned to the USA. A stalwart of the 303rd, 41-24605 was duly flown by no fewer than 17 separate crews up until it too was ferried back home in June 1944. The bomber suffered no major battle damage during its many missions, and was ultimately scrapped at Stillwater, in Oklahoma, in July 1945. The B-17 is depicted wearing the supposedly short-lived red surrounds to the star and bar marking. Units were given a month to paint out the red border, but examples such as this existed well into 1944. The odd medium green camouflage pattern applied to 41-24605 was not unique to this aircraft, as other ETO B-17s wore similar schemes during this period. Note also the two kill markings below the upper turret. The scrap view reveals the full bomb log that adorned KNOCK-OUT DROPPER.

6

B-17F-27-BO 41-24614 WE THE PEOPLE of the 364th BS/305th BG, flown by Lt Cliff Pyle, Grafton Underwood, November 1942

Assigned to the group on 22 August 1942, this B-17F was one of the aircraft flown by the 305th BG from the USA to England in October. At the controls for the epic transatlantic crossing was Lt (later Capt) Cliff Pyle, who reported to his ground-

crew upon arriving at Grafton Underwood that the bomber consistently lost power as it gained altitude. The cause of this problem proved difficult to locate, and the crew consequently named their troublesome aircraft SNAFU. However, after completing a couple of missions they decided that they did not like this name, so adopted WE THE PEOPLE instead. This sobriquet was recommended to them by the Gulf Oil Company, whose popular radio programme bore the same name. Enjoying a long career in the frontline, the aircraft (flown by Maj J C Price) led the first VIII BC night bombing mission on 8 September 1943, being one of five 422nd BS B-17s which joined RAF Bomber Command in a raid on the Boulogne area. During more than 30 missions WE THE PEOPLE never carried exactly the same crew twice, and no crewman was ever wounded flying in it. Removed from the frontline in May 1944, the aircraft was eventually flown back to the USA, where it was sold for scrap at Searcy Field on 31 July 1945. Shown with its waist and radio room gun positions closed, the profile also reveals a yellow dot aft of the single code letter 'R'. This was the position reserved for the 'marking of the day', which was adopted in 1943 in an effort to help AAF B-17 crews spot captured Fortresses that were attempting to infiltrate formations.

7

B-17F-27-BO 41-24619 of the 427th BS/303rd BG, Molesworth, Autumn 1943

Simply known as 'S For Sugar' due to its squadron code letter, this aircraft was assigned to the 427th BS/303rd BG at Kellogg Field, Michigan, on 26 August 1942. In November it was flown to Molesworth, in England, by Capt (later major, and CO of the 427th BS) Glenn E Hagenbuch, who also had the 427th BS's CO, Maj Charles C Sheridan (killed in action on 3 January 1943), aboard for the crossing. 41-24619 was the only bomber in the squadron at this time devoid of a nickname, although it did carry the unit's traditional 'Bugs Bunny' insignia on both sides of the nose. Col James H Wallace, as CO of the 303rd BG, chose 'S for Sugar' to lead the first group mission of the war when St Nazaire was bombed on 17 November 1942. Three months later legendary American journalist Walter Cronkite of the United Press news bureau rode as a passenger on the 26 February 1943 mission to Wilhelmshaven. On 14 May Capt Donald Stockton was killed in action piloting 'S for Sugar' during the raid on Kiel when a cannon shell exploded against his seat. Co-pilot Lt John C Barker then took control of the aircraft, and aided by flight engineer T/Sgt Roy Q Smith, succeeded in getting the aircraft safely back to base. 41-24619 was just beaten to the 50 mission mark by fellow 303rd BG B-17F KNOCK-OUT DROPPER on 16 November 1943, although unlike its group rival, this aircraft did not survive the war. On 11 January 1944 'S for Sugar', with Lt Thomas Lamarr Simmons' crew aboard, was shot down during the raid on the Focke-Wulf plant in

Osc|ersleben, in eastern Germany. This was the crew's third mission in the veteran bomber, and all ten of them successfully baled out.

8
B-17F-20-DL 42-3057 *BLONDE BOMBER* of the 322nd BS/91st BG, flown by 2Lt Wayne Murdock, Bassingbourn, January 1944
Like 'S for Sugar', this aircraft was lost on the Oschersleben raid on 11 January 1944 after suffering numerous 20 mm cannon shell hits both during the bombing run to the target and whilst trying to escape back across western Germany. The radio operator was killed during one of these attacks by *Jagdwaffe* fighters, which also set his compartment alight. The remaining nine crewmen successfully baled out, although the pilot was killed when his parachute failed to deploy. This was *BLONDE BOMBER's* 28th sortie since arriving in the UK on 28 March 1943, having flown over from the USA on the newly-opened southern ferry route via the Moroccan city of Marrakech. Issued to the 91st BG, 42-3057 flew its first eight missions as *Piccadilly Commando*, before being renamed by its new crew in late June. This profile shows how the aircraft would have looked in the weeks prior to it final sortie. Note the twin .50-cal mounting in the Plexiglas nose, and the deletion of the astrodome forward of the cockpit – the fitting for the latter is clearly visible, however.

9
B-17F-55-BO 42-29524 *"MEAT HOUND"* of the 423rd BS/306th BG, Thurleigh, Spring 1943
Accepted by the AAF on the last day of 1942, this aircraft was eventually assigned to the 423rd BS on 2 March 1943. After completing a number of missions with this unit it moved to Molesworth on 30 July to join the 303rd BG's 358th BS. On 26 January 1944, whilst returning from the Focke-Wulf plant at Oschersleben, this aircraft (manned by 2Lt Jack W Watson's crew) was attacked by enemy fighters, who shot out two of its engines. Realising the hopelessness of the situation, the pilot gave the bale out order, and the men evacuated the doomed bomber in a series of delayed jumps over the Netherlands. Co-pilot 2Lt C C David successfully evaded, three crewmen were killed and six others captured. Depicted in profile whilst still part of the 306th BG, *"MEAT HOUND"*, like *BLONDE BOMBER*, has the twin .50-cal Plexiglas mounting – note the red-painted blast deflectors fitted to the barrels of the Browning guns. The small secondary radio mast on the fin fillet is also clearly visible.

10
B-17F-60-BO 42-29591 *The Shamrock Special* of the 401st BS/91st BG, Bassingbourn, October 1943
Delivered to the AAF in January 1943, and in turn passed on to the 336th BS/95th BG at Alconbury in April of that year, this aircraft moved to Framlingham with the group the following month.

It completed just two combat sorties with the 95th (11 and 13 June), although on the latter mission one of the Eighth Air Force's gunner aces, Donald Crossley, was credited with his fourth and fifth kills. The bomber was then transferred to the 91st BG's 401st BS, where it saw much action both over Europe and at its own field – in the latter instance, it was hit by a battle-damaged Fortress (B-17F 41-24639 *The CAREFUL VIRGIN*) that landed without brakes at the end of a sortie in November 1943. The rear fuselage was written off in the accident, so the tail section of another B-17 with front-end damage was bolted to *The Shamrock Special*. It returned to combat on 30 December, and went on to complete a further 12 missions before returning to the USA in mid-1944. As this profile reveals, 42-29591 was unique within the 91st for boasting two pin-ups, the second artwork on the tail (nicknamed *Hollywood 337*) being painted by groundcrewman Jack Gaffney, who was also responsible for christening the B-17 *The Shamrock Special*.

11
B-17F-70-BO 42-29751 *Miss Abortion* of the 534th BS/381st BG, Ridgewell, December 1943
Originally assigned to the 338th BS/96th BG at Grafton Underwood on 19 April 1943, this aircraft transferred to the Ridgewell-based 381st BG on 7 December. Issued to the 534th BS, the bomber had been at its new base for just a matter of weeks when higher authority ordered that its unsavoury nickname be changed. 42-29751's crew duly obliged by re-christening the veteran B-17 *STUFF*. On 31 March 1944, after completing 21 combat missions, the bomber (with 1Lt Wayne G Schomburg at the controls) crashed just short of the runway at Ridgewell following a routine practice flight. All six men in the scratch crew, including T/Sgt Donald B Carr, who was a veteran of 20 combat missions, and Capt Paul H Stull Jr, the 534th BS's Engineering Officer, who was sitting in the co-pilot's seat, were killed.

12
B-17F-70-BO 42-29784 *"Smilin-Thrü* of the 545th BS/384th BG, Grafton Underwood, October 1943
Accepted by the AAF in mid-February 1943, this aircraft was delivered to the 305th BG's 366th BS at Chelveston on 18 May. It remained with the group until 11 September, when it transferred to the 534th BS/381st BG, although the bomber's stay at the group's Ridgewell base was to be a short one, for it moved on to Grafton Underwood, and the 545th BS/384th BG, on 4 October. Ten days later it was one of the many bombers badly damaged during the second Schweinfurt raid, the aircraft being successfully crash-landed by its pilot, 2Lt Erwin C Johnson, at Blayden, in Gloucestershire. It was broken up for scrap on the spot.

13
B-17F-70-BO 42-29815 *MIAMI Clipper* of the 322nd BS/91st BG, Bassingbourn, March 1943
Also delivered to the AAF in February 1943, 42-

29815 was initially issued to the 367th BS/306th BG on 20 April 1943. Named after the famous east coast railroad express train, *MIAMI Clipper* transferred to the 91st BG at Bassingbourn on 14 September, where prolific Eighth Air Force artist Cpl Anthony 'Tony' Starcer (of Bassingbourn's 441st Sub Depot) decorated the nose of the combat veteran. 42-29815 completed its last mission on 23 March 1944, after which it was flown back to the USA and eventually sold for scrap at Walnut Ridge on 9 January 1946.

14

B-17F-75-BO 42-29888 *"The Joker"* of the 532nd BS/381st BG, Ridgewell, April 1944
Surviving some of the most dangerous missions of the war, *"The Joker"* spent its entire frontline career with the 381st BG. Arriving at Ridgewell on 6 April 1943, the bomber became a permanent fixture within the 532nd BS until replaced by a B-17G in early May of the following year. In that time it successfully completed over 20 missions, and its gunners were credited with at least nine aerial kills. 42-29888 was flown back to the USA in August 1944 and sold for scrap three months later.

15

B-17F-75-BO 42-29923 *The LUCKY STRIKE* of the 532nd BS/381st BG, Ridgewell, late 1943
Arriving in the UK on 18 May 1943, this aircraft was originally assigned to the 364th BS/305th BG at Chelveston, where it was named *PAPPY'S HELLIONS III*. 42-29923 was transferred to Ridgewell on 11 September, and its new crew immediately re-named it *The LUCKY STRIKE*, complete with an artistic rendition of a cigarette packet. For some reason the aircraft only flew two combat missions with the group in four months, and on the second of these (on 4 January 1944) it was badly damaged over Kiel. *The LUCKY STRIKE's* pilot on this occasion, 2Lt Rowland H Evans, succeeded in nursing the bomber back to Norfolk, where he put it down at Cawston – two crewman were killed in the crash-landing, which wrote the B-17 off. Evans (a philosophy professor at Williams' College, in Massachusetts, before the war) survived the crash, only to be listed as missing in action on 22 February 1944 when, as part of 1Lt Lee W Smith's crew. His aircraft was one of six B-17s that failed to return from a raid on Bunde, in Germany.

16

B-17F-80-BO 42-29947 *WABASH CANNONBALL* of the 322nd BS/91st BG at Bassingbourn, early 1944
This aircraft was first assigned to the 100th BG at Podington on 8 May 1943, moving with the group to Thorpe Abbotts on 9 June. On 6 July 42-29947 transferred to the 322nd BS/91st BG at Bassingbourn, where Tony Starcer applied his Disney-inspired 'Goofy' nose-art (one of the few such artworks produced by the prolific Starcer). The bomber's name was inspired by an old West Virginian ballad, although who chose this sobriquet remains a mystery. The *'CANNONBALL* flew

its first mission on 14 July 1943, but had to abort the next three. With such a poor record, the aircraft could easily have become something of a 'jinx ship', but the B-17 turned the corner in August – it suffered no further aborts until February 1944. On 23 May David Hanst nursed the *'CANNONBALL* home from Berlin after flak had shot out the No 3 engine, which in turn caused the propeller to fly off, scattering debris through the side of the B-17. After 60+ missions, the last of which was flown on 25 July, the veteran bomber was transferred to the 303rd BG two days later, where it was used as a HQ 'hack'. 42-29947 returned to America in July 1945, where it was broken up for scrap.

17

B-17F-80-BO 42-29953 *Wolfess* of the 364th BS/305th BG, Chelveston, November 1943
This aircraft was first assigned to the 535th BS/381st BG on 25 April 1943, and subsequently completed ten missions with the group as *Man O'War*. On 22 August it was transferred to the 305th BG's 364th BS at Chelveston, being renamed *Wolfess* in the process. On 15 November the aircraft (flown by 2Lt Wetzel F Mays) was involved in a mid-air collision with B-17F 42-30666 near Newton Bromswold, in Northamptonshire. Both aircraft had just completed a group take-off and assembly, and were flying back across Chelveston airfield at 1000 ft, when *Wolfess* suddenly rose up and struck the underside of 42-30666, which was being flown by the 364th BS's Operations Officer, Capt Varney D Cline. The B-17s were each carrying a full fuel load of 1700 gallons, and the bombers violently exploded upon impacting the ground. All 21 crewmembers (including Varney Cline, who had completed his tour of missions and was about to be sent home) were killed.

18

B-17F-115-BO 42-30712 *MISS MINOOKIE* of the 323rd BS/91st BG, Bassingbourn, September 1943
Arriving at Bassingbourn fresh from the USA on 27 September 1943, this aircraft flew the first of its 22 combat missions on 8 October when the group was sent to bomb Bremen. On 21 February 1944 *MISS MINOOKIE*, with 1Lt Neal Ward and his crew aboard, was lost during an attack on the airfield at Achmer, the bomber being shot down by fighters near Luechtreigen, in Germany. Four crewmen were killed and a further six captured. This artwork shows how the bomber looked soon after it had arrived at Bassingbourn following the addition of Tony Starcer nose-art in the form of a topless, grass-skirted, castaway. This aircraft has faired nose gun positions and a field-modified aerial and mast under the bombardier's compartment.

19

B-17F-125-BO 42-30857 *My Devotion* of the 510th BS/351st BG, Polebrook, October 1943
Named after a popular song of the period, this late-production F-model (fitted with the same

Sperry A-1 upper turret as utilised by the B-17G, together with a faired nose position) was delivered to the 351st BG on 22 September 1943. The impressive nose-art worn by this aircraft was created by waist gunner Seymour Ziegler, who used a picture of a bathing beauty that he found in YANK magazine as a guide. He simply removed her bathing suit when creating his masterpiece, using his imagination to 'fill in the blanks'! 42-30857 was duly transferred to the 837th BS/487th BG, at Lavenham, on 16 July 1944 as part of the group's switch from B-24s to B-17s. Returned to the USA in December 1944, the bomber was sold for scrap at Altus on 6 August 1945.

20
B-17G-5-BO 42-31143 Satan's Lady of the 369th BS/306th BG, flown by Loy F Peterson, Thurleigh, October 1943

One of the first B-17Gs to arrive in the UK, this aircraft was issued to the 369th BG on 19 October 1943. Assigned to the crew of Loy F Peterson, Satan's Lady replaced their previous B-17F, which was named Satan's Mistress. Enjoying a long life with the group, 42-31143 gained the reputation of being a lucky aircraft, and numerous crews requested to fly it on their last missions. Peterson was at the controls of Satan's Lady on D-Day, and completed his own tour aboard this Fortress nine days later. By war's end the bomber had logged 112 missions without suffering a mechanical failure, and although shot up on numerous occasions, none of the myriad crewmen who flew in it were ever wounded. Passed to the 381st BG in May 1945, the aircraft returned to the USA in June 1945 and was sold for scrap at Kingman, in Arizona, the following November. This profile shows the bomber with an enclosed waist gunner's position, the distinctive chin turret synonymous with the G-model and green propeller hubs, denoting its assignment to the 369th BS. The nose-art is based on the same pin-up that inspired the artwork worn by My Devotion.

21
B-17G-5-DL 42-3524 Vonnie Gal of the 527th BS/379th BG, Kimbolton, June 1944

Although built at Boeing's Denver plant as a B-17F-75, this aircraft was fitted with the G-model's chin turret and longer faired nose, but retained the F-model's upper gun turret and open waist gun positions! Redesignated a B-17G-5, it arrived at Kimbolton for service with the 379th BG on 3 October. Initially issued to the 526th BS, the bomber was soon passed on to the 527th BS, where it was christened Vonnie Gal. A 'regular' with the squadron well into 1944, the aircraft completed 27 or 28 of its 50 missions manned by 1Lt Jack Lamont's crew. By July 1944 42-3524 was the oldest operational Fortress within the 379th, but its lengthy career with the group came to an end on the 20th of that month. The bomber was struck by flak just after its crew, led by 2Lt William F Moore, had released its bombs during a raid on Leipzig.

Running low on fuel, Moore chose to land at Payerne airfield, in Switzerland, where both his crew and his bomber were interned. Vonnie Gal was finally flown back from Switzerland to Burtonwood, in Lancashire, on 25 September 1945, where it was subsequently scrapped just weeks later.

22
B-17G-15-BO 42-31353 QUEENIE of the 322nd BS/91st BG, flown by Lt Bob Fancher, Bassingbourn, March 1944

Assigned to the 322nd BS on 20 December 1943, QUEENIE flew her first mission on Christmas Eve, when the 91st BG attacked a V1 site at Andres, in France. The bomber was allocated to Lt Bob Fancher's crew six days later, and during their first mission together QUEENIE suffered heavy battle damage over Ludwigshafen. The aircraft later participated in the first large daylight raid on Berlin (on 6 March 1944), with Fancher's co-pilot, Lt Louis Lahood, flying in the left-hand seat on this occasion. Passed on to 1Lt James F Purdy's crew when 42-31353 was transferred to the 323rd BS in early April, the aircraft was downed by flak over 'Big B' on the 29th of that same month. Only half the crew survived. Like numerous other 91st BG B-17s, this aircraft featured Starcer nose-art – in this instance modelled on the September 1943 Varga calendar girl. Turning to the mechanics of the aircraft, QUEENIE boasted a revised Sperry A-2A ball turret with modified glazing, flat sides and exterior mountings.

23
B-17G-15-BO 42-31367 Chow-hound of the 322nd BS/91st BG, flown by 1Lt Jerold Newquist, Bassingbourn, April 1944

Delivered to the 91st BG on 25 January 1944, this aircraft was in turn issued to the 322nd BS's 1Lt Jerold Newquist and crew, who decided on its unique nickname because they liked to 'fight to eat and eat to fight'. Tony Starcer painted a 'Pluto'-like cartoon hound riding a bomb on the nose of the B-17. Chow-hound flew its first mission on 29 January, and Newquist completed 22 of his 25 combat missions in this aircraft. Lt Maynard Frey's crew added another 13 missions to its tally, including one on D-Day. 1Lt Jack Thompson's crew then flew a further 13 missions in the bomber until it fell victim to a direct flak hit on 8 August when en route Caen, in France – a shell penetrated the centre fuselage of the aircraft before exploding, breaking the B-17 in two. None of the crew survived. This profile shows the aircraft fitted with blast deflectors for the chin guns, which were attached so as to protect the longer Plexiglas nose of the B-17G. Aside from the nose-art, individual crew 'legends' were also painted beneath some of the crew stations on this aircraft; "Newky Newquist" Head Chief below the pilot's window, "Jumpin Joe Bentzel" beneath the upper turret and "The judge in Charge, Callaway" below the port waist gun position.

24

B-17G-20-BO 42-31585 *MOUNT 'N RIDE* of the 323rd BS/91st BG, flown by Lt Roman Maziarz, Bassingbourn, February 1944

Flown into Bassingbourn on 1 February 1944, this aircraft was quickly adorned with Starcer artwork in the form of that month's *Esquire* Varga calendar girl. This aircraft and Lt Roman Maziarz's crew flew their first mission, to Avord, in France, just four days after the bomber had been delivered to the 91st. On the 6th Lt Doyle Bradford's crew took over the aircraft, and they continued to fly it without incident until 16 March, when it lost both inboard engines to flak during a raid on Lechfeld airfield. Bradford struggled over the Alps to Switzerland, where he put the bomber down safely at Dübendorf. Both the crew and its bomber were interned until the end of the war, *Mount 'N Ride* finally being flown back to Burtonwood on 8 October 1945, where it was scrapped.

25

B-17G-25-BO 42-31713 *SNAKE HIPS* of the 327th BS/92nd BG, Podington, August 1944

Another February 1944 arrival for the Eighth Air Force, this aircraft was assigned to the 92nd BG on the 11th of that month. It survived unscathed in the deadly skies of western Europe until the 24 August mission to Merseburg, when the bomber took an 88 mm flak round directly in the bomb-bay while on the run in to the target. Miraculously, the bombs did not explode, although the burst tore out the right side of the bomb-bay, reduced the radio room to a shambles, punched a gaping hole in the fuselage and severed aileron and elevator controls. Ball gunner, Sgt Gordon V Wescott, was fatally wounded by the explosion, and he died a few minutes later. Pilots 2Lts John Bosko and Curt H Koehnert fought to keep the bomber aloft as *SNAKE HIPS* fell out of control, losing about 2000 ft a minute. During the descent the hydraulic system caught fire and fluid spread over the floor of the fuselage and the catwalk in the bomb-bay. Engineer, S/Sgt Peter W LaFleur, tried to put out the blaze with a fire extinguisher, and when this ran dry, he tore out the flaming insulation from the walls of the bomb-bay with his bare hands. Although most of the aircraft's ordnance had been blown away by the initial impact of the flak round, five bombs remained in the shattered bomb-bay, and the crew knew full well that they could explode at any minute – their arming wires had been torn out and the vanes were slowly turning. One bomb was already fully armed. Bombardier, S/Sgt Jerome E Charbonneau, who had at one time served as an armament chief, worked perilously on the slippery, burning catwalk, removing the live nose fuse from the armed bomb, and directing the waist gunner and radio operator as they dealt with the tail fuses and spinning vanes. Rendered harmless, the bombs were finally pried loose with a screwdriver. Bosko and Koehnert flew the crippled B-17 out over enemy territory at low altitude, and midway over the North Sea two engines went dead through fuel starvation. The bomber finally made it to Woodbridge (the nearest available airfield), where Bosko ordered the crew to bale out, before he succeeded in safely landing one of the most badly-damaged B-17s to make it back to the UK. It was reduced to scrap just days later.

26

B-17G-30-BO 42-31863 *Miss "B" Haven* of the 614th BS/401st BG, Deenethorpe, March 1944

Built in Denver, this B-17 was delivered to the 401st BG on 6 February 1944. It had an engine knocked out by flak over Augsburg 19 days later, the bomber returning to base minus the propeller from its starboard inner engine. After this early setback, *Miss "B" Haven* went on to complete almost 12 months of uninterrupted frontline service with the 614th BS until damaged beyond repair during a mission to Cologne on 6 January 1945. The bomber was declared fit only for scrapping upon its return to Deenethorpe, and duly passed on to the 2nd Strategic Air Depot (SAD) at Little Staughton for salvaging on 18 February.

27

B-17G-25-VE 42-38083 *MAN O WAR II HORSEPOWER LTD* of the 322nd BS/91st BG, Bassingbourn, April 1944

Assigned to the 91st BG on 1 February 1944, this aircraft was the last of three Fortresses in the group to carry the name of the famous Triple Crown winner *MAN O WAR HORSEPOWER LTD*. The first example was B-17G 42-37987, which Lt William Burtt crash-landed following its one and only mission, to Frankfurt, on 29 January 1944. Having adorned the original '*HORSEPOWER LTD* with an intricate equestrian nose-art, Tony Starcer repeated this artwork on 42-38083, with a slight rearrangement of titling on the scroll. The second aircraft completed 77 combat missions before enemy action finally claimed it on the 2 November raid on Merseburg. Of the crew, only the pilot, 1Lt Leroy Hare, and his co-pilot, bombardier and navigator survived. This profile reveals that 42-38083 was one of the few olive drab B-17s in the 91st BG to be adorned with the group's full late-war markings, including a red fin, horizontal stabilisers and wing tips.

28

B-17G-40-BO 42-97058 *SCORCHY II* of the 359th BS/303rd BG, Molesworth, April 1944

Arriving at Molesworth on 27 March 1944, this aircraft was one of the first natural metal B-17s issued to the 303rd BG. It became a stalwart of the group, remaining in the frontline until lost on 21 January 1945 during the raid on Aschaffenburg, in Germany. Manned by 2Lt Richard E Tasker's crew, the bomber was the victim of a mid-air collision over Rottweil – only one crewman succeeded in baling out. The artwork shows the aircraft wearing the late-war tail markings employed by the group from August 1944 until war's end. These effectively comprised a full red surround for the white identification triangle in the middle of the fin, with the yellow '2' above the black 'C' (formerly dark blue on olive drab Fortresses) denoting assignment to the 359th BS.

29
B-17G-40-BO 42-97061 *GENERAL "IKE"* of the 401st BS/91st BG, Bassingbourn, April 1944
One of the 91st BG's most famous bombers, this aircraft had initially been assigned to the 457th BG at Glatton on 13 March 1944. However, it was transferred to the 401st BS/91st BG three days later, and soon after its arrival at Bassingbourn, legendary artist Tony Starcer got to work creating one of his most photographed pieces of work – the portrait of Gen Dwight D Eisenhower, Supreme Commander, SHAEF. Unusually, he applied the nose-art to both sides of 42-97061, whilst Cpl Elvis White was responsible for the distinctive lettering that accompanied both artworks. On 11 April, during a ceremony held at Bassingbourn, Gen Eisenhower christened his namesake with a bottle of Mississippi River water which had been brought to the ETO by a pilot who had planned to drink it upon the completion of his tour, but who had been lost on a mission. *GENERAL IKE* completed its first operational sortie (to Schweinfurt) on 13 April, and on 29 May the B-17 led the 91st BG to Poznan, in Poland, on the longest daylight bombing raid of the war up to that time. On the *'GENERAL's* 65th mission, a windmilling No 3 propeller sheared off and sliced into the nose-art, but miraculously no-one was even scratched. *GENERAL IKE* survived the war, having flown at least 32 group leads, and was eventually scrapped in the USA in late 1945. This profile reveals that the bomber had a grey-painted chin turret left over from its earlier OD days, red propeller hubs denoting its assignment to the 401st BS, and a retrofitted Cheyenne tail turret.

30
B-17G-45-BO 42-97272 *DUCHESS' DAUGHTER* of the 359th BS/303rd BG, Molesworth, June 1944
Allocated to the 303rd BG on 9 April 1944, 42-97272 had completed 30+ missions when it was written-off on 6 July in an accident at Molesworth. Pilot 2Lt I J Judy was at the controls when his co-pilot inadvertently flipped up the landing gear switch instead of the flap retraction toggle during the rollout after landing! The subsequent accident considerably damaged the aircraft, and the chances of the co-pilot ever becoming a first pilot or a first lieutenant. 42-97272 was salvaged by the 2nd SAD the next day.

31
B-17G-45-BO 42-97385 *SHADY LADY* of the 601st BS/398th BG, Nuthampstead, August 1944
An April 1944 arrival at Nuthampstead, this aircraft boasted yet more artwork inspired by Varga's work in *Esquire* magazine – in this instance, the June 1943 gatefold, entitled 'Something for the

Boys'. *SHADY LADY*, manned by 2Lt Warren J Wade's crew, failed to return from the Ludwigshafen raid of 8 September, when the pilot was forced to crash-land the aircraft at Rechicourt-le-Chateau, in France, after she developed a mechanical fault. Three crew were killed in the violent landing, two evaded capture and four were made PoWs. What remained of 42-97385 was duly destroyed by American fighters before the Germans could recover the wreckage.

32
B-17G-20-VE 42-97557 *Mercy's MADHOUSE* of the 359th BS/303rd BG, Molesworth, mid-1944
This aircraft was initially delivered to the 482nd BG in February 1944, being amongst the first 24 B-17Gs in the ETO to boast a factory-fitted H_2X radar scanner in a semi-retractable radome. Dubbed a *Mickey* ship by the crews that flew it, the bomber was initially issued to the 482nd BG on 5 February. It was then transferred to the 422nd BS/305th BG on 20 March. Few B-17s had H_2X in the first half of 1944, and 42-97557 was regularly passed from one group to the next within the 1st Air Division. Although nominally assigned to the 544th BS/384th BG from 4 August 1944 until war's end, it is seen here wearing the markings of the 358th BS/303rd BG. The veteran bomber made the returr trip to the USA in June 1945 and was subsequently sold for scrap at Kingman the following December.

33
B-17G-35-VE 42-97880 *LITTLE Miss Mischief* of the 324th BS/91st BG, Bassingbourn, September 1944
Assigned to Lt Joe Bessolo's crew within the 91st BG's 324th BS upon its arrival at Bassingbourn on 15 June 1944, this aircraft was quickly embellished with a Starcer artwork – the crew studied 25 of the artist's George Petty-inspired centrefolds before they chose the *Esquire* pin-up seen here. Pilot Bessolo went on to complete all except the last of his 28 combat mission tour on this aircraft. Incredibly, on 15 October 1944 Lt Paul McDowell managed to bring *LITTLE Miss Mischief* back to Bassingbourn despite the bomber having suffered a direct flak hit over Cologne, which had cleaved the B-17 almost in half. The only way the group's maintenance men in the 441st Sub Depot could fix the aircraft was to cut it in two and graft the rear, olive drab, half of B-17G 42-31405 (which had previously served as *Walleroo Mark II* with the 359th BS/303rd BG until written off in a forced-landing on 7 August 1944) onto the forward fuselage of 42-97880. The 'new' bomber went on to complete a further 15 missions, and survive further damage following a crash-landing at Bassingbourn on 4 April 1945 – the bomber had lost an engine en route to Fassberg airfield, causing its pilot to abort the mission. Repaired once again, 42-97880 was transferred to the 306th BG at Thurleigh in May 1945. Shown prior to its rebuild, this profile of *LITTLE Miss Mischief* reveals small, non-standard, touches such as a single squadron-coloured pro-

peller boss and a replacement OD engine cowling panel. The aircraft also features a modified aerial fit synonymous with late-build 91st BG B-17Gs, retrofitted staggered waist gunners' positions and an enclosed radio room gun position devoid of the actual weapon itself.

34

B-17G-35-DL 42-106992 *Baby Lu* of the 612th BS/401st BG, Deenthorpe, April 1944
Delivered to the 401st on 16 April 1944, this aircraft featured nose-art that was inspired by Varga's 'Pistol Packin Mama', published in *Esquire* magazine in early 1944. After surviving a year in the frontline with little more than a couple of minor flak holes, 42-106992 successfully carried out a forced-landing on the continent on 19 April 1945. Subsequently repaired, *Baby Lu* was able to return to the USA three months later, where she was assigned to the 4185th Base Unit at Independence, before being sold for scrap at Kingman on Christmas Day 1945.

35

B-17G-35-DL 42-107027 *HIKIN' FOR HOME* of the 322nd BS/91st BG, Bassingbourn, January 1945
Originally assigned to the 401st BS at Bassingbourn upon its delivery to the 91st BG on 7 April 1944, the bomber supposedly arrived on-base already wearing the name *Annie* or *Anne* below the cockpit on the pilot's side. It then transferred to the 322nd BS, where it was re-named *The BLOODY BUCKET*, although this name was officially ordered to be removed by senior officers within the Eighth, who objected to the profanity! Renamed for a third time, *HIKIN' FOR HOME* led a seemingly charmed life in the frontline, although it did suffer its far share of battle damage. On 14 February 1945, during a raid on Dresden, the bomber was badly shot up, and then six days later its pilot carried out a forced-landing at Denain, in France. *HIKIN' FOR HOME* subsequently became the first B-17 to be repaired on the continent and returned to its group. After VE-Day, the bomber transferred to the 384th BG at Istres, in France, where it was used to shuttle displaced persons and PoW back from North Africa. On 31 December 1945 *HIKIN' FOR HOME* (which had by then flown over 125 missions) was salvaged by the Ninth Air Force.

36

B-17G-35-DL 42-107112 *SLEEPY TIME GAL* of the 532nd BS/381st BG, Ridgewell, April 1944
Sent to the 381st BG on 6 April 1944, this aircraft was adorned with nose-art inspired by Varga's 'Patriotic Gal', which graced the gate-fold in that month's *Esquire* magazine. Whilst with the group the aircraft was regularly flown by Lt David R Morgan's crew, and by war's end, the bomber had completed more than 47 missions. Flown back to the USA at the end of May 1945, *SLEEPY TIME GAL* was eventually sold for scrap at Kingman in November of that year.

37

B-17G-65-BO 43-37516 *TONDALAYO* of the 406th BS(H)/305th BG, Cheddington, February 1945
The 422nd BS had become the Eighth Air Force's first night bombing squadron in September 1943, and this aircraft was assigned to the specialist unit on 4 June 1944. By this time the unit had abandoned night bombing in favour of night leaflet drops. Just weeks after *TONDALAYO* arrived on the unit, it changed its designation to the 858th BS(H) and moved stations to Cheddington – on 11 August further changes saw the squadron become the 406th BS(H). Although repainted matt black overall in order to render the aircraft less visible at night, the bomber still retained the group's white identification triangle and full colour markings! *TONDALAYO* dropped tonnes of leaflets across Europe up until the night of 4 March 1945, when it was shot down in error off Clacton by British shore batteries that had opened fire on a German intruder detected in the same area. Squadron CO, Lt Col Earle Aber, was at the controls on this fateful night, and after ordering the crew to bale out, he and his co-pilot, 2Lt Maurice Harper, remained at the controls in a desperate bid to reach the emergency field at Woodbridge. Despite their best efforts, *TONDALAYO* crashed into the sea in flames, killing both men.

38

B-17G-70-BO 43-37707 *MADAME SHOO SHOO* of the 324th BS/91st BG, Bassingbourn, September 1944
Initially assigned to the 91st BG's 322nd BS on 28 June 1944, this aircraft was later transferred to the 324th BS. Performing the bulk of its missions with the latter unit, the B-17 arrived on the squadron already adorned with a Starcer pin-up – this artwork was inspired by the languorous lady in Milton Caniff's famous cartoon strip of the time, *Male Call*. *MADAME SHOO SHOO* was lost in the last weeks of the war when Lt David Hanst's crew failed to return from the mission to bomb the marshalling yards at Stendal on 8 April 1945. Suffering severe battle damage near the target, the pilot carried out a forced-landing on the continent and the aircraft was abandoned as damaged beyond repair.

39

B-17G-40-DL 44-6009 *FLAK EATER* of the 364th BS/305th BG, Chelveston, September 1944
Issued to the 305th BG on 17 May 1944, this aircraft saw much action as 'WF-J', but after sustaining battle damage on a mission on 12 September 1944, *FLAK EATER* was repaired and re-coded 'WF-U'. On 4 December 1944 44-6009 failed to return to Chelveston following another raid on Germany, being put down instead in an emergency landing on a newly-created airstrip on the continent. Repaired once again, the aircraft survived the war having flown in excess of 28 missions. The veteran bomber was transferred to the 351st BG on 23 May 1945, before returning to the USA in June. *FLAK*

EATER was scrapped at Kingman the following December.

Back cover
B-17G-50-VE 44-8152 *MISS IDA* of the 748th BS/457th BG, Glatton, October 1944

Received by the 457th BG on 22 September 1944, this aircraft was fitted out as a PFF platform with H$_2$X radar in a retractable opaque dome in place of the ball turret. On 5 April the aircraft was designated as the lead ship for the raid on Ingolstadt, although during taking off in the pre-dawn darkness, it suffered an engine fire and crashed near the base. Full of fuel and ordnance, the B-17 exploded when it hit the ground, killing nine of its ten-man crew, including the 748th BS's CO, Maj Ed Dozier. The only survivor was navigator, Lt Willing Meng, who was thrown clear during the initial impact. Although severely injured, he eventually made a full recovery.

BIBLIOGRAPHY

Andrews, Paul M & Adams, William H. *Heavy Bombers of the Mighty Eighth*. Eighth Air Force Museum Foundation Project Bits & Pieces, 1995

Birdsall, Steve. *Pride of Seattle - The Story of the first 300 B-17Fs*. SquadronSignal, 1998

Birdsall, Steve. *Fighting Colors - B-17 Flying Fortress*. SquadronSignal, 1986

Birdsall, Steve & Freeman, Roger A. *Claims to Fame - The B-17 Flying Fortress*. Arms & Armour, 1994

Bowden, Ray. *Plane Names & Fancy Noses - the 91st BG(H)*. Design Oracle Partnership, 1993

Bowman, M W. *Four Miles High*. PSL, 1992

Bowman, M W. *Flying To Glory*. PSL, 1992

Bowman, M W. *Castles In The Air*. PSL, 1984

Bowman, M W. *Boeing B-17 Flying Fortress*. Crowood, 1998

Caldwell, Donald. *The JG 26 War Diary volume one 1939-42*, Grub Street, 1996

Caldwell, Donald. *The JG 26 War Diary volume two 1943-45*, Grub Street, 1998

James, Good Brown. *The Mighty Men of the 381st - Heroes All*. Publishers Press, 1984

Freeman, Roger A. *The Mighty Eighth*. MacDonald, 1970

Freeman, Roger A. *Airfields of the Eighth - Then and Now*. After the Battle, 1978

Freeman, Roger A. *Mighty Eighth War Manual*. Jane's, 1984

Freeman, Roger A. *The Mighty Eighth In Art*. Arms & Armour, 1996

Freeman, Roger A with Osborne, David. *The B-17 Flying Fortress Story*. Arms & Armour, 1998

Havelaar, Marion H with Hess, William N. *The Ragged Irregulars of Bassingbourn*. Schiffer Military History, 1995

MacKay, Ron. *381st Bomb Group*. SquadronSignal. 1994

McDowell, Ernest R. *Flying Fortress in Action*. SquadronSignal, 1987

Smith Jnr, Ben. *Chick's Crew - A Tale of the Eighth Air Force*. privately published, 1978

Stapfer, Hans-Heiri. *Strangers In A Strange Land*. SquadronSignal, 1988

Strong, Russell A. *First Over Germany - A History of the 306th BG*. Hunter Publishing, 1982

Weal, John. *Osprey Aircraft of the Aces 9 - Focke-Wulf Fw 190 Aces of the Western Front*, Osprey Aviation, 1996